Royal Trivia

Royal Trivia

Sarah Edmunds

PIATKUS

This book is dedicated to my mother, the most ardent of
Royalists and the loyalist of subjects. May I justify
the pride she has always shown in her children.

Copyright © 1990 Sarah Edmunds

First published in 1990 by
Judy Piatkus (Publishers) Ltd
5 Windmill St, London W1P 1HF

British Library Cataloguing in Publication Data
Edmunds, Sarah
   Royal trivia: all you ever wanted to know about the Royal Family.
   1. Great Britain. Royal families
   I. Title
   941. 08580922

ISBN 0–7499–1001–1

Designed by Paul Saunders
Edited by Kelly Davis
Cartoons by Jonathan Pugh
Cartoon on page 94 reproduced with the permission of Punch Publications

Phototypeset in 11/13 Linotron Times Roman by
Phoenix Photosetting Ltd, Chatham, Kent
Printed and bound in Great Britain by
Mackays of Chatham PLC, Chatham, Kent

CONTENTS

INTRODUCTION

They may be the British Royal Family, but they have fans in every country of the world. Though the media report their every move, Britain's first family remain beyond the reach of the majority of their subjects. Perhaps this is why we long to know what their lives are really like . . .

I have been a dedicated Royal-watcher since early childhood, and was prompted by an American friend to write this book. My motivation was curiosity – curiosity about the mundane (Which is the Queen's favourite TV soap opera?); the quirky (Which Royal always has a cooked breakfast?); and the ceremonial (What strain of rose was used in Diana's wedding bouquet?).

If you too find it difficult to satisfy your craving for Royal trivia, then you may want to gobble up this book whole. Those with less voracious appetites may simply wish to nibble away a little at a time. However you choose to sample this dish, the author wishes you Bon Appétit!

Sarah Edmunds
Wiltshire, 1990

THE PATTER OF TINY ROYAL FEET

*R*oyals *have been born in some unusual places. From Buckingham Palace to St Mary's Hospital, Paddington, from Clarence House to the dining table of a Royal residence in foreign parts, the manner of their arrival has sometimes been far from regal!*

Princess Anne broke with centuries of tradition when she appeared, pregnant with her son Peter, during the Queen's Silver Jubilee celebrations. Before this, expectant Royal mums tended to remain cloistered within one residence or another. Even Queen Elizabeth II was merely reported as being 'in an interesting condition . . .'

★　★

When discussing clothes for Princess Diana's first pregnancy, the fashion designer Bruce Oldfield commented:

‹You should be proud of your growing figure. You could be carrying a future King of England. ›

★　★

Comments on Royal births:

‹I wouldn't recommend the experience to anyone. ›
>　—**Captain Mark Phillips,** after the birth of his son Peter.

‹Fantastic experience. Absolutely fantastic. ›
>　—**Prince Charles,** after the birth of Prince William.

'If there has to be a man outside my bedroom door, I hope it's someone we know.'
>—**The Queen Mother,** on the now defunct tradition of having the Home Secretary present at Royal births.

'What, you mean I can't have any more fun in bed?'
>—**Queen Victoria,** on being told that Princess Beatrice should be her last baby.

★ ★

Who said . . . ?
'My chief claim to fame seems to be that I am the father of Princess Elizabeth.'
>—**The Duke of York, and future George VI.**

★ ★

Princess Diana

On twins:
'I couldn't cope with a brace.'

On motherhood:
'It's hard work and no pay.'

To a friend:
'If I have another boy and you have another daughter, we'll swap.'

★ ★

Who described the newborn Princess Diana as 'a superb physical specimen'?
>—*Her father*

★ ★

Who said . . . ?
'I'm getting fed up waiting for it to arrive.'
>—**The Queen,** to a crowd of well-wishers a few hours before the birth of Princess Beatrice.

★ ★

The Duke and Duchess of York's second child, Princess Eugenie Victoria Helena of York, was born on 23 March 1990 at 7.58 pm and weighed in at 7lbs 1½oz (3.24kg).

★ ★

The bookmakers' favourite choice of first name for Princess Beatrice of York's little sister was Charlotte.

★ ★

Mr George Pinker, surgeon-gynaecologist-in-waiting to the Queen, has delivered nine Royal babies:

Alexander, Earl of Ulster Lady Davina Windsor Lady Rose Windsor	Children of the Duke and Duchess of Gloucester
Lord Frederick Windsor Lady Gabriella Windsor	Children of Prince and Princess Michael of Kent
Peter Phillips Zara Phillips	Children of The Princess Royal and Captain Mark Phillips
Prince William of Wales Prince Harry of Wales	Children of the Prince and Princess of Wales

★ ★

Fathers who have been present at Royal births:
Prince Albert, Prince Michael of Kent, Prince of Wales, Duke of York, Captain Mark Phillips.

★ ★

On the birth of Prince Charles, the Duke of Edinburgh gave his wife a huge bouquet of deep pink carnations. They were waiting by her bed when she woke from the anaesthetic.

★ ★

When Anne, the Princess Royal, left St Mary's Hospital, Paddington, after the birth of her son Peter, nursing staff presented the new baby with a large, cuddly, Paddington Bear, complete with red wellies and floppy hat.

Princess Elizabeth and her sister Margaret were pushed about by their nannies in a cast-iron pram, complete with Royal monogram on the side panels.

★ ★

Following the birth of her daughter at Clarence House, both the Queen (then Duchess of Edinburgh) and the baby Princess were looked after by the Royal nurse, Sister Rowe.

★ ★

All four of the Queen's children were kept as close to their mother as possible during their early weeks. During the day they slept in a crib while she worked in her room; Prince Philip would join his wife there for meals. The crib itself was made of dark wood, and was hung with pastel and white gauzy fabric and lace.

★ ★

The Queen and Prince Philip took it in turns to bath their children, official duties permitting.

★ ★

Royal mothers who chose to breastfeed their babies:
Queen Elizabeth the Queen Mother, Queen Elizabeth II, Princess Anne, Princess Diana, Duchess of York (reputedly).

★ ★

The children of the Prince and Princess of Wales, and the son of the Princess Royal, were baptised by Archbishops of Canterbury, but Zara Phillips was baptised by the Dean of Westminster. The Music Room at Buckingham Palace is now the usual venue for these Royal occasions, and for the official photocall afterwards.

★ ★

Princess Margaret was the first member of the Royal Family to be born on Scottish soil since Charles I in 1660. She was born at Glamis Castle, and not at Buckingham Palace or Clarence House as is often claimed.

Princess Beatrice of York's godparents:

David, Viscount Linley –
Eleventh in line to the throne and the only Royal on the list.

The Duchess of Roxburghe –
She and her husband own Floors Castle, where Prince Andrew proposed to Miss Sarah Ferguson; their daughter Rosanagha was a bridesmaid to the Yorks.

Peter Palumbo –
Friend of the Ferguson family and Chairman of the Arts Council. He had a row with Prince Charles, who referred to Palumbo's Mansion House scheme as a 'glass stump'.

Mrs Carolyn Cockerall –
The Duchess of York's ex-flatmate. Married to an Old Etonian, she is cousin to Anne Beckwith-Smith, lady-in-waiting to the Princess of Wales.

Mrs Gabriella Greenall –
A skiing friend of the Duchess of York.

★　★

Princess Anne's godparents include the Queen Mother, Earl Mountbatten of Burma and Princess Alice of Greece.

★　★

Prince William was christened on the Queen Mother's eighty-sixth birthday.

★　★

Prince Harry was christened in Christmas Week, 1984.

★　★

Princess Beatrice of York was baptised by the Archbishop of York, at the Chapel Royal, on 20 December 1988. (All Royal babies wear the Honiton lace robe, which is kept in a hermetically sealed container in between trips to church; the lily font is also always used.)

★　★

The Queen was born at 17 Bruton Street, London, and not 145 Piccadilly, as many people think.

Royals whose births caused some consternation:

Eddie, Duke of Clarence, the Queen's great uncle, was born nearly three months prematurely. In fact, his mother, Princess Alexandra, failed to reach full term in any of her six pregnancies.

Duke of Edinburgh was born on the dining table of 'Mon Repos', the family home on the Greek island of Corfu.

The future George VI chose the anniversary of Prince Albert's death to enter the world.

★   ★

Blue for a boy:
When Prince Charles was born, baby-blue spotlights washed over Buckingham Palace, and thousands of people who had gathered outside the palace gates sang 'Go to Sleep' to the tune of Brahms' _Lullaby_.

★   ★

When Princess Margaret was born, a forty-one gun salute was fired in the Tower of London, and the bells of St Paul's Cathedral rang out in celebration.

KEEPING IT IN THE FAMILY

The Royal family tree is extensive and not entirely British, with members of the Romanian, Russian and other foreign Royal families taking their place in the queue for accession to the throne.

One of Princess Diana's ancestors, Robert Spencer, was the second Earl of Sunderland. He inveigled himself into the position of Chief Adviser to Charles II, James II and William III, by changing loyalties and religion with each succeeding monarch. Many of the valuables at Althorp were acquired by him.

★　★

The Duke and Duchess of Gloucester's son is the Earl of Ulster.

★　★

The Queen is a distant relative of George Washington.

★　★

Princess Diana is a distant relative of Ronald Reagan.

★　★

The Princess of Wales and the Duchess of York both have older sisters called Jane.

★　★

Queen Elizabeth the Queen Mother had two older sisters called Rose and Mary. She also has a niece called Jean and a sister-in-law named Betty.

★　★

Whose coat of arms includes the bumble bee, symbolising industry and hard work?
The Duchess of York's.

★　★

To avoid confusion, the correct ways of referring to the two most senior Royal ladies are the Queen (Queen Elizabeth II), and Queen Elizabeth (The Queen Mother).

★　★

Her Majesty the Queen is also Duchess of Edinburgh.

★　★

Prince Charles is heir apparent to the title of Duke of Edinburgh.

★　★

Princess Diana is only the ninth Royal lady to bear the title, 'Princess of Wales', in its 700-year history.

★　★

Princess Michael of Kent was the only member of the Royal Family to address the late Duchess of Windsor as 'Your Royal Highness'.

★　★

The Princess of Wales and the Duchess of York could quite correctly be addressed as Princess Charles and Princess Andrew respectively – though Fergie finds the idea of being called 'Andrew' highly amusing.

★　★

Princess Anne did not want any further titles, until her mother made her Princess Royal in recognition of the work she has done for the Save the Children Fund.

WHAT'S IN A NAME?

Countless people have named their children after members of the various royal families – how about Zog for a boy?

Queen Victoria's christening descended into farce as arguments raged across the font – between godparents, the Archbishop of Canterbury and William IV – over what the infant should be called. Three of the proposed names were eventually dropped, so Britain didn't get a Queen Georgiana after all.

★   ★

The full Christian and maiden name of the Queen Mother's mother was Nina Cecilia Cavendish-Bentinck.

★   ★

When the Queen gave birth to her second child in 1950, she was able to do something which had been vetoed when she herself was born: she named her daughter Anne. In 1926 and 1930, the then Duke and Duchess of York were sternly informed by George V that Anne was not a suitable choice for either of their daughters.

★   ★

Highly unlikely names of Royals:
King Zog and Queen Geraldine of Albania.

15

When Princess Anne's second baby was due, bookmakers backed the name Elizabeth to win. They were somewhat surprised when her names – Zara Elizabeth Anne – were announced. 'We'd never have guessed,' commented one bookmaker ruefully.

* *

Names of the Duchess of York's brother and sisters:
Jane Louisa (26.8.57) Andrew Frederick Victor John (07.9.77) Alice Victoria (26.12.80) Eliza (09.10.85).

* *

Was the name of the Duke and Duchess of York's first baby a choice prompted by family politics? In her speech at the State Opening of Parliament, the Queen hinted at the greatly improved relations between Britain and Spain. Beatrice was the name of King Juan Carlos's great-grandmother.

* *

First names Diana wanted for her first baby:
Oliver, Arthur . . .
And the names he got:
William Arthur Philip Louis.

* *

Possible names for future children of the Prince and Princess of Wales:
George, Georgina, Nicholas, Philip, Caroline.

* *

Possible names for future children of the Duke and Duchess of York:
Henrietta, George, Christian, Mary.

* *

Andrew and Fergie originally chose the name Sophie for their first child. However, the Queen was reported (in the US press) to have rejected their choice as being 'too foreign' – despite Andrew having Christian as a middle name.

Royal middle names:

The Queen – *Alexandra Mary*

The Princess Royal – *Elizabeth Alice Louise*

Peter Phillips – *Mark Andrew*

Zara Phillips – *Elizabeth Anne*

The Princess of Wales – *Frances*

The Duchess of York – *Margaret*

The Duke (Edward) of Kent – *George Nicholas Paul Patrick*

The Duchess (Katherine) of Kent – *Lucy Mary*

David, Viscount Linley – *Albert Charles*

Lady Sarah Armstrong-Jones – *Frances Elizabeth*

Princess Alexandra (Mrs Angus Ogilvy) – *Helen Elizabeth Olga Christabel*

★ ★

The Duke of York's middle names are Albert Christian Edward (or 'ACE', as Fergie said in her pre-wedding TV interview).

★ ★

Surnames from the Queen's side of the family:
d'Abreu, Windsor, Bowes-Lyon, Levenson-Gower, Cambridge, Elphinstone, Harewood.

★ ★

During the Great War of 1914–18, the people of Britain and their allies developed an almost pathological hatred of anything German – including German Shepherd and Dachshund dogs – and those with the remotest connection to 'the Hun' suffered all sorts of abuse.

There was therefore a frantic search amongst those members of the Royal Family who bore Teutonic names and titles, anxious to change them to something more in keeping with the public mood. The Battenbergs (all except Prince Philip's mother), simply transposed the direct English translation onto their surname, and became Mountbatten. Their princely titles, however, had to go, as these had been conferred in Germany: hence they became Marquises.

Eventually, someone realised that it would be hard to find a name more English than Windsor. On 17 July 1917, it was decreed that George V and his descendants would bear the name Windsor. The Queen later added that for *her* descendants, the name would be Mountbatten-Windsor.

Back in Germany, Kaiser Wilhelm could not resist a dig at his English cousins, declaring one evening to family and friends that he was going to see a performance of Shakespeare's 'The Merry Wives of Saxe-Coburg-Gotha'.

★ ★

Nicknames applied to the Royals:

Charley's Aunt – Princess Margaret's joke against herself

'Our Val', Princess Pushy, Princess Porky, Rent-a-Princess – Princess Michael of Kent

Dynasty Di, Shy Di, the Duchess – Princess of Wales

Bloody Pom – Prince of Wales, by Geelong classmates

The Frog Prince – Prince Charles, by his wife

Fergie – Duchess of York

Phil the Greek – Duke of Edinburgh

Wills – Prince William, by his father

Beetroot, Queen Bea – Princess Beatrice of York, by the press

Discount Linley – David, Viscount Linley

Melons, Royal Raver – Lady Helen Windsor

Mo, Action Girl – Marina Ogilvy

Queen Mary's pet name for her infant grand-daughter Elizabeth was '*The Bambino*'.

★ ★

Princess Alexandra's family nickname is '*Pud*'. She was born at Christmas.

★ ★

The Canadian nation's nickname for the Queen Mother is QE2.

★ ★

In the African dialect spoken in the Sudan, Princess Anne is known as '*Mtoto ya Queenie*'.

★ ★

Private Eye's nicknames for the Royals:
Brenda – The Queen   *Yvonne* – Princess Margaret

★ ★

More Royal nicknames:
The World's Youngest Old Fogey, Action Man – Prince Charles
Miss Piggy – The Queen
Craggy Face – Prince Philip
The Royal Floosie – Princess Margaret

★ ★

Who referred to Queen Victoria as 'Our queer old dean'? Doctor Spooner, of Spoonerism fame. He meant, of course, to propose a toast to 'Our dear old Queen'.

★ ★

Aliases used by the Duke of York:
Andrew Edwards – On a school trip to France.
Mr Cambridge – Flying to Mustique with Koo Stark.
Mr Newman – Flying back from Mustique – without Koo Stark.

YOUNG ROYALS

Like children everywhere, Royal offspring can be angelic, endearing and cute . . . they can also be naughty and infuriating – the throwers of toys and tantrums.

Who said . . . ?
‘Can't my sister join? You see, she does so love getting dirty.’
> —**Princess Elizabeth.** She had just been made a Girl Guide but her younger sister, Princess Margaret, had to wait until she was old enough.

★　★

Of whom was it said . . . ?
‘She's so outrageous, one can't help but encourage her.’
> —**Princess Margaret,** by her grandmother, Queen Mary.

★　★

Princess Elizabeth wore the uniform of a Girl Guide when she 'signed on' at the Labour Exchange in 1942. Under wartime legislation, everyone had to register on their sixteenth birthday, either for war work or for military service. The future Queen joined the ATS when she was eighteen.

As children, the Queen Mother and her brother David made a secret den in the garden of the family home of St Paul's Walden Bury, Hertfordshire. In it they would hide caches of sweets, chocolate and occasionally . . . illicit cigarettes.

★ ★

All well-bred children in Hanoverian Britain were expected to imitate the upright poise of their elders. To train them to 'keep their chins up', a sprig of holly would be pinned to their clothing; a drooping chin thus resulted in uncomfortable prickling. Queen Victoria herself suffered this form of domestic torture, and said how much she hated 'holly days'.

★ ★

When she was very young, so little was seen of the future Queen Victoria that strange stories began to circulate. One such snippet, repeated at society dinner parties, was that she did 'unspeakable things' with her asparagus! (I wonder what?)

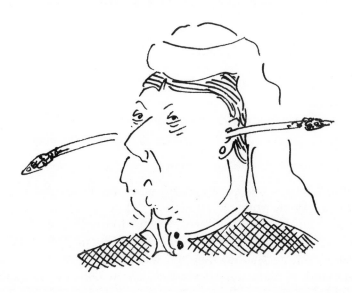

Favourite toys:

Princess Elizabeth and Princess Margaret – Model horses with groomable manes, tails and coats, and miniature tack.

Princess of Wales – Dolls, soft toys, a Victorian doll's tea set, her baby brother.

Princesses Elizabeth and Margaret and their Lascelles cousins – Miniature Welsh cottage

Anne, Princess Royal – Her pony, Greensleeves, her pedal car

Andrew, Duke of York – Miniature Aston Martin

Prince William – Plastic bathtime whale, toy cars

Prince Harry – Colouring books, slide and pet rabbit

Prince Charles – Toy trumpet, pedal car

★   ★

Who said . . . ?
‹It's all scratchy. ›
　　　　—A three-year-old **Prince Charles** to his nurse, referring to a new tweed coat, which was then returned to the Royal seamstress to have the silk lining lengthened.

★   ★

Who said . . . ?
‹I can read. I can sew. I can wash myself. ›
　　　　　　　　　　　—**Princess Anne,** aged five.

★   ★

Prince Charles was very pleased when his new baby sister arrived. As she grew old enough to toddle around, he would try to steady her tottering steps. But the future Princess Royal had soon had enough of big brother's well-intentioned protectiveness – if he tried to take her hand, she would wrench it away and, if that didn't deter him, she would deliver quite hefty smacks!

'He's perfectly capable of doing that himself.'
>   —**The Duke of Edinburgh** to a Buckingham Palace
>   footman, who had been about to close a door
>   behind a small Prince Charles.

★ ★

Prince Andrew, Duke of York, was the fattest of the Queen's
four babies. He has had a tendency to chubbiness ever since,
appearing slimmest in his early twenties.

★ ★

Who pretended . . . ?
That his mother was a housewife, his father a wealthy farmer,
and that his name was Andrew Edwards?

Prince Andrew, on a school trip to France. His hosts didn't
believe him either.

★ ★

Of whom was it said . . . ?
'I have never known a boy sit so still.'
>   —**Prince Edward** aged five, by his grandmother the
>   **Queen Mother.** His own mother described him as
>   'the quietest of my children'.

★ ★

While still at prep school, Prince Edward was often called 'the
Glum Prince' because he never seemed to smile for photographers. In common with many children of the same age,
Prince Edward merely wanted to hide . . . his corrective
dental brace.

★ ★

When Charles, Anne, Andrew and Edward were very small
the Prime Ministers of the day were only too willing to comply
with the Queen's request: could they possibly make arrangements for their twice-weekly meetings with her to be held
later in the evening? Otherwise, she would be busy when it
was time to read her children's bedtime stories.

Lady Diana Spencer and her younger brother Charles used to be invited to Sandringham House for tea, with the Queen's two youngest children. On one such occasion, a three-year-old Prince Edward managed to coat himself in honey from the tea table.

★   ★

When Lady Diana Spencer was told not to play her hi-fi system so loud at Althorp she didn't just turn the volume down. She dismantled the wiring so it wouldn't play at all.

★   ★

Who said . . . ?
It was a great room for playing bears in.
　　　　　—**Earl Spencer,** on the nursery at Althorp.

★   ★

Garry! Garry!
　　　　　—**Prince William** could not pronounce 'Granny' as a
　　　　　toddler; he was calling the Queen.

★   ★

I'm looking for something he won't be able to break.
　　　　　—**Princess Diana,** choosing a birthday present for
　　　　　Prince William.

★   ★

Have you seen William anywhere? It's bathtime and as usual he's disappeared.
　　　　　—**Princess Diana** to two journalists who were at
　　　　　Highgrove to interview Prince Charles.

★   ★

The coats worn by Prince William and Prince Harry are exact copies of those worn by the Prince of Wales as a child – right down to the unlikely pink colour choice. Many of Prince Charles's baby and toddler clothes have survived, and it is almost certain that these will have been handed down.

Prince William and Prince Harry also have miniature Barrack Dress uniforms, presented to them by the Parachute Regiment, of which their father is Colonel-in-Chief.

★ ★

In 1987, Prince Harry of Wales was given the part of an elf in his school's Christmas play. The following year, the little Prince was promoted to shepherd. During the 1988 production, he had to whisper the lines to a small female member of the cast, who had 'dried'. Prince Harry's parents thought their son's acting was *'Splendid!'*.

★ ★

The Duchess of York purchased a video camera after Princess Beatrice was born, so that she could film the baby and keep the Duke up to date on her latest developments during his long absences at sea.

★ ★

Princess Anne chose pale green and white as the colour scheme for her first baby's nursery; Princess Diana chose comic frog motifs.

★ ★

For his first official photographs, Peter Phillips wore a hand-knitted angel top, presented to the newborn son of Princess Anne by the British magazine *Woman's Own*.

★ ★

Who said . . . ?
‘Oh, they're not Royal. They just have an aunt who happens to be Queen. ’
> —**Princess Margaret,** of her children.

BACK TO SCHOOL

Cheam, Gordonstoun, Wetherby, Eton and Geelong Grammar are all schools which have educated Royals. The Queen Mother maintains that life itself is the best teacher, and she's probably right.

The Queen Mother's formal education – that is, in a classroom with other girls of the same age (and class) – lasted just two months, at Miss Goff's Day School, in Marylebone High Street, London. The rest of her education took the form of tuition by her mother, Countess Strathmore, and by a governess.

★ ★

The Queen and Princess Margaret were both educated at home by a series of governesses. Their parents, the then Duke and Duchess of York, did consider the possibility of a boarding school education for the two princesses, but George V was not at all impressed by the idea and it positively horrified Queen Mary. When she became heir to the throne, Princess Elizabeth had extra lessons, on instruction in the unwritten British Constitution and history, given by Sir Henry Marten, the Provost of Eton. The Duchess of York taught her daughters to play the piano, to sketch and paint, to be knowledgeable about country ways as well as the protocol and etiquette of court life. Their father's groom, Owen, was in charge of riding lessons and pony care.

★ ★

Reading matter for the young Princess Elizabeth consisted not only of classics, such as *Black Beauty* and *Wuthering Heights*, but also the French masterpieces of Molière, Phèdre and George Sand, and weighty tomes entitled *National Expenditure Before the 1939 War* and *The Evolution of a Self-Governing Dominion*.

★ ★

Prince Philip was Captain of the cricket and hockey teams at Gordonstoun. As a cadet at the Royal Naval College, Dartmouth, he was awarded the Eardley-Howard-Crocket Prize and the King's Dirk.

★ ★

Prince Charles's first school report at Hill House School, Knightsbridge:

Reading	*Very good indeed.*
Writing	*Good. Firm, clear, well-formed.*
Scripture	*Shows keen interest.*
Geography	*Good.*
French	*Shows promise.*
Latin	*Made a fair start.*
Art	*Good and simply loves drawing and painting.*
History	*Loves this subject.*
Arithmetic	*Not very keen.*

★ ★

Who said . . . ?
‘Well, at least he hasn't run away yet. ’
　　　　—**Prince Philip,** when asked how Prince Charles was settling into Gordonstoun School.

★ ★

Who ordered Prince Charles to get off his bike?
> —Mr George Hales, porter at Trinity College, Cambridge.

* *

At Cambridge University, Prince Charles first studied archaeology and anthropology, and later, history.

* *

When was Prince Charles attacked by a set of Scottish bagpipes?
He 'wrestled' with the rampant plaid during the Footlights Review at Cambridge University. His parents were sitting in the front row.

Prince Charles readily admits that his French is of quite a low standard. His sister had the same problem but then she enrolled at the Berlitz Language School for a crash course in French conversation, and passed with flying colours.

* *

As a pupil at Benenden School between 1963 and 1968, the Princess Royal gained six O-levels (including an A grade in English Literature) and two A-levels (including a Merit in Geography).

★ ★

Who said . . . ?
'At school we knitted squares; they weren't always square, but they went to make up blankets of sorts!'
> —**The Princess Royal,** on her early unofficial help for the Save the Children Fund.

★ ★

Andrew, Duke of York's, education:

Buckingham Palace, private tutor (shared with his cousin Viscount David Linley)

Heatherdown Preparatory School

Gordonstoun School

Royal Naval College, Dartmouth

Royal Naval College, Greenwich

★ ★

As the Queen worked at her desk, the pre-school age princes, Andrew and Edward, played at her feet. Visitors were sometimes surprised to see a child's blackboard and easel in the room – the Queen used it to teach her youngest children to write and tell the time.

★ ★

Prince Edward studied archaeology and anthropology, with history as a later option, at Cambridge University – an identical course to that taken by his eldest brother.

★ ★

Princess Diana's education:

Gertrude Allan 'Ally' – Governess at Park House, Sandringham.

Silfield School, King's Lynn – Aged 7 to 9 years.

Riddlesworth Hall, Norfolk – Aged 9 to 14 years.

West Heath School, Kent – Aged 14 to 16 years.

Institut Alpin Vidamanette, Switzerland – She lasted six weeks and then came back, dreadfully homesick.

★ ★

Princess Diana is teaching her sons, William and Harry, to play the piano.

★ ★

The Duchess of York's education:

Mrs Laytham's Kindergarten, Englefield Green ('for the children of the gentry').

Hurst Lodge School, Charters Road, Sunningdale, Ascot. The Duchess of York has six O-levels and three A-levels.

Queen's Secretarial College, Queensberry Place, South Kensington – She graduated after nine months with 90 words per minute shorthand, 39 words per minute typing.

★ ★

At Hurst Lodge, the Duchess of York was house prefect of 'de Valois House', and joint head girl (an honour shared with Fenella, daughter of showbiz star Ted Rogers).

ROYAL ROMANCES

The press lost count of the beautiful young women seen in the company of Prince Charles and, to a lesser extent, Prince Andrew. Through the ages matters of the heart have caused joy, sorrow and scandal. Read on . . .

First meetings between Royals and their future spouses:

The Prince of Wales was present at the christening of Lady Diana Spencer.

Princess Elizabeth first met Lieutenant Philip Mountbatten on a visit to the Royal Naval College, Dartmouth; he was detailed as the young princesses' escort.

The future George VI sat next to five-year-old Lady Elizabeth Bowes-Lyon at a children's tea party. She gave him the cherry off her cake.

Captain – then a mere Lieutenant – Phillips regularly competed at the same equestrian events as his future wife.

★　★

Princes of Wales who fell in love 'easily' (but not always suitably): Edward VII, the Duke of Windsor, Prince Charles.

★　★

When asked how her husband had proposed to her, Princess Alice, Dowager Duchess of Gloucester, replied, 'I think he just muttered it as an aside during one of our walks.'

Ronald Ferguson proposed to the Honourable Mrs Shand-Kydd, Princess Diana's mother, when she was seventeen.

★   ★

Who said . . . ?
We spent all our married lives getting into other people's beds.
> —**Lord Louis Mountbatten** of Burma, on his marriage to Edwina Ashley.

★   ★

I can't imagine my parents making love.
> —**Prince Andrew,** in an interview broadcast on national radio.

★   ★

They're too inter-related.
> —A comment made on the proposed marriage of Princess Elizabeth and Lieutenant Mountbatten. The speaker was Chips Channon, a Royal commentator of the thirties and forties, and a member of Edward and Mrs Simpson's circle.

★   ★

Miss Suzannah Constantine was badly injured on a date with Viscount David Linley – she fell out of his open-top Mercedes as it moved off at speed. They both denied that there had been a lovers' tiff.

★   ★

Breakfast-time was an absolute riot.
> —**Prince Charles,** describing the morning a supposedly 'official' statement appeared in the British press, announcing his imminent betrothal to Princess Marie-Astrid of Luxembourg.

❛I must take up the Muslim religion and have lots of wives. ❜
—**Prince Charles,** during a trip to India just before his engagement to Lady Diana Spencer was announced.

★ ★

Who described Prince Charles as . . . ?
❛highly sexed ❜
—His ex-valet, the late Stephen Barry.

★ ★

And who said of Princess Diana . . . ?
❛She has a history, but no past. ❜
—Barbara Cartland, amongst others.

Previous escorts of Prince Charles:

Davina Sheffield – Daughter of a wealthy landowner.

Laura Jo Watkins – Daughter of US naval officer.

Lady Jane Wellesley – Daughter of Duke of Wellington.

Lucia Santa Cruz – His first real love. Daughter of Chilean Ambassador to London – but a constitutionally unsuitable Roman Catholic.

Lady Charlotte Manners – Aristocrat.

Rosie Clifton – Colonel's daughter.

Lady Leonora Grosvenor – Sister of the Duke of Westminster; married Earl of Lichfield, but has since divorced.

Lady Jane Grosvenor – Duchess of Roxburghe, sister of Lady Leonora Grosvenor. Applied for a divorce from her husband in March 1990.

Lady Victoria Percy – Aristocrat.

Rosie Bagge – Colonel's daughter.

Georgiana Russell – Sister of one of Charles's university friends.

Lady Sarah Spencer – Eldest sister of the Princess of Wales. Now married to Neil McCorquodale, and has three children.

★ ★

Although the Princess Royal and Mark Phillips are now separated, their two children still provide a great measure of family feeling. Divorce is unlikely in the short term. However Princess Margaret's initial estrangement from the Earl of Snowdon met with strong denials from the Palace that a divorce was in the offing, and yet barely two years later the divorce was announced.

★ ★

Ex-girlfriends of Prince Andrew:

Carolyn Seaward – Ex-Miss United Kingdom.

Koo Stark – Actress and photographer.

Vicki Hodge – Model.

Catherine Rabbett – Actress and model.

Carolyn Herbert – Daughter of the Queen's racing manager, and a friend of Princess Diana.

Kim Deas – Model.

Clare Park – Model turned photographer.

★ ★

Prince Andrew's first girlfriend was Jenny Wooten, a sixth-form pupil at Gordonstoun School.

★ ★

Fergie's first serious boyfriend was Old Etonian Kim Smith-Bingham.

★ ★

Who said . . . ?
Of course an attractive girl of twenty-six will have had previous boyfriends.
—**The Queen Mother,** during a family meeting to discuss the 'suitability' of Sarah Ferguson.

★ ★

He's a fantastic husband, actually. My rock.
—**The Duchess of York,** in 1989.

★ ★

They met on the polo field, of course. Where else does one meet people?
—**Mrs Susie Barrantes** (Sarah Ferguson's mother), on the Duke and Duchess of York.

Princess Margaret's first serious love affair, with Group Captain Townsend, war hero and equerry to her father, was ill-fated from the beginning as Townsend was a divorcee and therefore 'unsuitable'.

★　★

An accomplished actress, mimic, singer and musician, Margaret was attracted to the theatrical world. From there it was but a short step to the arts in a wider sense – painting, cinema, photography. Antony Armstrong-Jones was a leading member of the sixties' artistic set. Margaret had found love again. Their two children, David (Viscount Linley – he will eventually inherit his father's title, which was bestowed by the Queen on his marriage to Margaret) and Lady Sarah Armstrong-Jones, arrived soon after the wedding. The now Earl of Snowdon was in growing demand for design commissions and glossy magazine photography. His work, by its very nature, took him away frequently.

★　★

Possessiveness has been blamed for the final breakdown of the Snowdon marriage, along with a large dash of jealousy. Snowdon's name became linked to that of Lucy Lindsay-Hogg, and rumours were fanned following the crash of Snowdon's car. 'Who was the mystery woman passenger?' screamed the press.

★　★

Margaret's most famous subsequent escort was Roddy Llewelyn, now happily married and the father of two girls.

★　★

‘God grant the companion a better Prince, then we would soon be rid of her!’
> —**George V,** referring to Mrs Simpson, in reply to an aide's comment, 'God send the Prince a better companion.'

The Duke of Windsor would never believe that his brother, George VI, had been other than cruel in allowing the Duchess of Windsor only the title 'Her Grace', rather than 'Her Royal Highness'. In fact, there were good reasons for the King's decision. If she had been granted Royal status, Mrs Simpson could, in theory, have divorced the ex-king and returned to England, still demanding the rights of a Royal Duchess. It also followed that the Duke could have demanded the same title and recognition for any future wife.

★ ★

'You should erect a statue to her for saving us from Edward.'
    —Historian A. L. Rowse, of Mrs Simpson, to two visiting Americans from Baltimore, at Stratford-upon-Avon, 1988.

★ ★

In her youth, Queen Victoria had a crush on Lord Melbourne, and things came to such a pass that the poor man was terrified at being alone with her. Fortunately, Prince Albert replaced the noble lord in Victoria's affections.

★ ★

Despite their intense love for each other, Prince Albert and Queen Victoria sometimes had very loud and emotional rows – often concerning the manner in which their offspring should be raised. On one such occasion, Prince Albert stormed off and locked himself in the bedroom. Queen Victoria followed, banging on the door and demanding to be let in, shouting 'This is your QUEEN!' Eventually, she changed her plea: 'Please, Albert, let me in.' 'Who is asking?' enquired the Consort. 'Your wife,' replied the Queen. Albert then let her in.

WEDDING BELLS

It may be held at St Paul's Cathedral or Westminster Abbey, but the marriage service is the same for a Royal as it is for a commoner. It's just a little more public . . .

Who said . . . ?
'I'm afraid I won't ever see her again.'
> —**Earl Spencer,** on the engagement of his daughter Lady Diana to the Prince of Wales.

* *

'I got the news through the loo door.'
> —Carolyn Bartholomew (née Pride), friend of the Princess of Wales, describing how her flatmate Lady Diana Spencer broke the news that she was to marry Prince Charles.

* *

Over half a million people swarmed into London's Hyde Park for the public pre-wedding celebrations in honour of Charles and Diana. A magnificent firework display took place to the accompaniment of Handel's *Water Music*. Sadly, Lady Diana herself was not able to attend. She had to remain at Clarence House with the Queen Mother and watch the display on television. She was also told to 'have an early night'.

When Princess Alexandra of Denmark became engaged to Prince 'Bertie' of Wales in 1862, her engagement ring was a band of gold set with stones, the initials of which spelled out 'Bertie'; the first stone was a beryl.

★ ★

Princess Diana's engagement ring came from Garrards. It features a huge sapphire surrounded by fourteen large diamonds. There was no time to have the size of the ring band altered before the press photocall at Buckingham Palace, and it slipped up and down her finger when she moved her hand.

★ ★

The Duchess of York's engagement ring was chosen by Andrew, Duke of York. He stunned customers when he walked into Garrards and asked to speak to the manager – he and Sarah Ferguson had already inspected trays of rings brought to the Palace by various Royal jewellers. The huge cabuchon ruby, surrounded by ten diamonds, was chosen to match Sarah's red hair.

★ ★

Lady Elizabeth Bowes-Lyon decided upon a white rose wedding. Not only was the bride all in white, with a white bouquet, but so were her eight bridesmaids. The white rose is the emblem of the House of York.

★ ★

The silk used for the Queen's wedding dress had to be imported from China – Japanese silk was vetoed as unpatriotic so soon after the Second World War.

★ ★

The Duchess of Kent wore a dress designed by John Cavanagh for her 1961 wedding in York Minster.

★ ★

David and Elizabeth Emanuel, designers of Princess Diana's wedding dress, say they gain inspiration from watching old movies on TV, and that their ballgowns 'border on the erotic'. As they worked on the wedding dress of the century, all scraps of material and working designs on paper were incinerated at the end of each day.

★ ★

The lace on Princess Diana's wedding dress was Carrickmacross lace. It had belonged to Queen Mary and formed the 'something old' part of her outfit. Her ivory silk wedding slippers were made by Clive Shilton of London's Covent Garden.

★ ★

The sashes worn by Princess Diana's bridesmaids were chosen to match the golden yellow of the Mountbatten roses.

★ ★

Good luck symbols of two royal brides:

Princess Diana – David Emanuel sewed a tiny, diamond-studded gold horseshoe into the hem of her wedding dress.

Duchess of York – A blue bow was stitched onto the silk undies she wore beneath her bridal gown.

★ ★

The Duchess of York's wedding dress was made, appropriately, from duchess satin.

★ ★

Designers of Royal wedding dresses:
Norman Hartnell – The Queen
Susan Small – Princess Royal
The Emanuels – Princess of Wales
Lindka Ceirach – Duchess of York

★ ★

Jane Packer designed the bouquets and flower arrangements for the Yorks' wedding, which were then made up by Longmans the florists. Peach was the main colour theme.

Princess Diana's bridal bouquet included five types of flowers and three varieties of greenery: Mountbatten roses, stephanotis, white freesias, lily of the valley, odontoglossum orchids, ivy leaves, and sprigs of Queen Victoria's myrtle and veronica, still growing where she planted them after her own wedding, at Osborne House. She used cuttings taken from Balmoral.

★ ★

Where Royals have married:

Queen Victoria and Prince Albert – Chapel Royal, St James

Edward VII and Princess Alexandra – Chapel Royal, St James

George V and Queen Mary – Chapel Royal, St James

George VI and Queen Elizabeth – Westminster Abbey

Duke and Duchess of Windsor – Chateau de Candé

Queen Elizabeth and Prince Philip – Westminster Abbey

Edward, Duke of Kent, and Duchess of Kent – York Minster

Princess Anne and Captain Mark Phillips – Westminster Abbey

Prince Charles and Princess Diana – St Paul's Cathedral

Duke and Duchess of York – Westminster Abbey

★ ★

There were 6,750 policemen on duty for Princess Elizabeth's 1947 wedding, not counting the 450 plain clothes officers, 300 city constables and 600 special constables.

★ ★

It took twenty minutes for the Glass Coach to drive Lady Diana Spencer and her father to St Paul's Cathedral for her marriage. It was drawn by two Windsor Greys, named Lady Penelope and St David, and driven by senior coachman Richard Boland.

The Duchess of York was the ninth Royal bride to marry in Westminster Abbey this century. The nine were:

Princess Patricia of Connaught	1919
Mary, Princess Royal	1922
Duchess of York	1923
Princess Marina of Kent	1934
The Queen and Prince Philip	1947
Princess Margaret	1960
Princess Alexandra of Kent	1963
Princess Anne	1973
Miss Sarah Ferguson	1986

★ ★

Television coverage of Andrew and Sarah's wedding day commenced at 6.15 am in Britain.

★ ★

Who said . . . ?
‹She took my breath away. ›
> —**Major Ferguson,** when he first saw his daughter dressed for her Abbey wedding.

★ ★

When Prince William of Gloucester was page to Princess Elizabeth and Prince Philip, he tried to pre-empt the balcony appearance of the bride and groom. Three times he had to be retrieved by his nanny, but he finally managed to open the balcony doors, and enjoyed the cheers of thousands before being removed again.

★ ★

Princess Anne, when she married Mark Phillips in 1973, chose her youngest brother, Edward, as page, and her cousin, Lady Sarah Armstrong-Jones, as her sole bridesmaid. Royal observers expressed both surprise and disappointment at the small number of bridal attendants. The Princess, however, wanted to keep her wedding as near to a normal 'family wedding' as possible.

Princess Diana, before her marriage, was bridesmaid to both her sister Sarah and her sister Jane.

★ ★

Prince Philip took the role of substitute father when Princess Margaret married. He walked her up the aisle and 'gave her away' at the altar. The Prince, contrary to newspaper reports of the time, sided sympathetically with his sister-in-law over the Townsend affair.

★ ★

At the wedding of the Duke of Edinburgh's parents, Princess Alice was so confused by the complicated rites of the Greek Orthodox church that she inadvertently said 'No', when asked if she took Prince Andrew to be her husband.

★ ★

Witnesses to the marriage registration of Prince Charles and Princess Diana:

The Queen, Prince Philip, the Queen Mother, Prince Andrew, Prince Edward, Princess Anne, Lady Sarah Armstrong-Jones, Ruth, Lady Fermoy, Earl Spencer, the Honourable Mrs Shand-Kydd.

★ ★

Princess Elizabeth and Prince Philip did not meet with 100 per cent joy when their betrothal was announced; many people thought Philip was a German, and thus did not make a suitable Consort so soon after the Second World War.

★ ★

Prince Philip's wedding speech:
I am proud. Proud of my country and my wife.

Princess Elizabeth's wedding speech:
I ask nothing more than that Philip and I should be as happy as my father and mother have been, and Queen Mary and King George before them.

Eighty million Americans listened to the live wedding broadcast of Princess Elizabeth and Prince Philip.

★   ★

When the Prince and Princess of Wales emerged from St Paul's Cathedral after their wedding, the peal of a dozen bells from the north-west tower was the signal for every other church in the City of London to ring out in unison. All over the country, churches followed suit.

★   ★

Andrew and Sarah's 1986 Royal wedding was celebrated by the Poet Laureate, Ted Hughes, who wrote 'The Honey Bee and the Thistle' in honour of the occasion.

★   ★

Six bands played the ceremonial music for the wedding of Princess Anne and Captain Mark Phillips: the Royal Marines, the Coldstream Guards, the 3rd Battalion Light Infantry, the Metropolitan Police, the Central Band of the Royal Air Force, and the Band of the Scots Guards.

★   ★

Hymns chosen by Andrew and Sarah for their wedding:
'Praise to the Lord, the Almighty, the King of Creation'
'Lead Us, Heavenly Father, Lead Us'
'Come Down, O Love Divine'.

★   ★

For Princess Elizabeth and Prince Philip's Wedding Breakfast in 1947, the bride's father, George VI, chose partridge, as it was one of the few unrationed foods. The plates, cutlery and vases gracing the fifteen tables were all gold.

★   ★

Menu from the Prince and Princess of Wales's Wedding Breakfast:

Brill with Lobster Sauce

Chicken Breasts stuffed with Lamb Mousse
Selection of Fresh Vegetables

Fresh Strawberries and Cornish Cream
Wedding Cake
Vintage Krug Champagne

★ ★

Two wedding gifts for Anne and Mark:
18-carat gold candlesticks from President and Mrs Nixon.
A Morris Minor car bearing the numberplate '1 Ann' from Nottinghamshire County Council.

Before leaving Broadlands to await the Royal honeymoon couple in 1947, the daughters of Earl Mountbatten of Burma laid out a selection of popular dance records for Elizabeth and Philip to play.

Though Her Majesty prefers plain white bedlinen, on her honeymoon she had to settle for pink, crêpe-de-chine embroidered sheets and pillowcases. She declared them 'beautiful'.

★ ★

Wedding Night Supper of Princess Elizabeth and Prince Philip:

Potato Soup

Roast Chicken and Bread Sauce
Vegetables

Ice-cream
Coffee

. . . served on a small table before the fire. The meal ended at 10.30 pm and the lights of the newly-weds' suite were seen to go out at 11 pm.

★ ★

Estate workers were startled when, following their wedding night at Broadlands, the new Princess of Wales enjoyed sleeping in . . . while the Prince rose, had a hearty English breakfast (of sausages, eggs, bacon, kidneys and kedgeree) and went fishing on the River Test.

★ ★

The Princess Royal and Captain Mark Phillips spent their honeymoon aboard the Royal Yacht *Britannia*, cruising in the Caribbean.

★ ★

Part of Princess Diana's trousseau was a diaphanous pale peach nightdress and negligée. She also took a bright scarlet swimsuit on her honeymoon.

HAPPY FAMILIES

By Royal Command, Easter, Christmas and some other holidays are spent with the monarch – whether they like it or not, and even if they don't like each other!

Life in the residences at Balmoral, Sandringham and Buckingham Palace runs on very prescribed lines – Her Majesty does not like change. For instance, at Balmoral, there is the Scottish pipe major who, resplendent in kilt, sporran and bearskin, plays his bagpipes under the window at breakfast-time. He doubles as a film projectionist in the evenings; each of the Queen's homes has one room which can be converted to a mini-cinema.

★　★

At Gatcombe Park, Highgrove House and the Wales's Kensington Palace apartments, the children often appear when they are least expected – they are not automatically ushered from the room when visitors arrive. There are toys and children's drawings lying around, Wellington boots stand by the door, and in the Princess Royal's home a couple of large dogs are as much a part of the furnishings as a table or sofa.

★　★

Princess Diana has a large 'No Smoking' sign in her private sitting room at Kensington Palace.

In a corner of her private sitting room in Clarence House, the Queen Mother has an electric kettle and a selection of kitchen canisters, so that she can brew herself coffee or tea (using teabags), without bothering a member of staff. She also prefers to drink tea and coffee from a mug, rather than a cup and saucer.

★   ★

Who said . . . ?
‹Don't forget, my dear, you have to reign all afternoon. ›
    —**The Queen Mother** to her eldest daughter, while she pondered whether to have a second glass of wine with lunch.

★   ★

At Royal picnics at Balmoral, cutlery, plates, glasses and cold food – such as smoked salmon and smoked quail – are unpacked from traditional hampers. Plaid travelling rugs are arranged round a central tablecloth, and 'The Wagon' is awaited. This is an invention of Prince Philip's. The separate steel compartments ensure that dishes which are supposed to be served hot do indeed arrive that way from the kitchens of the Royal residences.

★   ★

Princess Diana is a light sleeper, and requires absolute quiet to ensure a good night's rest. Prince Charles, on the other hand, can 'sleep through anything'.

★   ★

‹I always call him "Sir". ›
                —**Earl Spencer,** on his Royal son-in-law.

★   ★

When Princess Alexandra married Angus Ogilvy in 1962, a souvenir programme was published. It included a family tree – but excluded the Duchess of Windsor.

★   ★

Who said . . . ?
❝I was bloody shabbily treated. ❞
    —**The Duke of Windsor,** referring to the events of 1936.

★   ★

In 1976, the Queen Mother attempted to make peace with the Duchess of Windsor. On a visit to Paris, the Duchess refused a visit from the Queen Mother; later, she also turned away the huge basket of pink roses sent by her Royal sister-in-law, saying, 'We never even exchanged Christmas cards'. A strange comment from the Duchess, as the discovery of the Windsor's personal papers in the Duke's bathroom in 1988 proved, for there, amongst the photographs and menu cards, were wads of greetings cards from all the Royals.

★   ★

The Queen Mother did not wholly approve of Prince Charles spending so much time in the company of his 'Honorary Grandfather', Lord Louis Mountbatten, whose bisexual habits had been the talk of high society.

★   ★

Royal men who enjoyed bathing their own babies:
George V, Prince Philip, Prince Charles.

★   ★

In 1983, Prince Charles was rebuked, both publicly and privately, for spending so much time at home with Prince William, thus making himself unavailable for public engagements. Since Prince William and Prince Harry have started school, however, the Prince of Wales has maintained a high, caring profile.

In a family photograph which appeared in a Silver Jubilee souvenir brochure, Prince Andrew can be clearly seen poking his tongue out at Captain Mark Phillips.

★ ★

Did you know that . . .
Roddy Llewelyn *always* addressed Princess Margaret as 'Ma'am', even when away from public gaze?

And that . . .
George V and Queen Mary, the Queen Mother and Princess Margaret all have in common the habit of 'dressing for dinner' in the evening, whether guests are expected or not?

And . . .
At the wedding of Princess Mary of Teck to the Duke of York, the bride's parents were not allowed to sit at the same table as their daughter . . . their Royal rank wasn't high enough.

★ ★

There are points of etiquette to be observed on greeting the Queen, but after the obligatory bow or curtsey, her children and their spouses kiss her. Her grandchildren run towards her with outstretched arms, to be greeted warmly by 'Granny'. When the Queen and Princess Margaret were children, their father waived the curtsey rule – but Queen Mary insisted that they should observe correct protocol with her.

★ ★

Which Royal has been smacked in public by her mother?
Zara Phillips.

★ ★

The inhabitants of the 'Royal Triangle' – the Prince and Princess of Wales, Prince and Princess Michael of Kent, and the Princess Royal and her children – may not be renowned for their 'chumminess'. However, the family nannies regularly take the youngest Royals to visit one another, to play and have tea, whilst the nannies chat.

Royal nannies:

Mary Peterson (committed to an asylum for the mentally unbalanced); Lalla (Charlotte Bill) – Both for George V's children.

'Bobo' (later the Queen's Dresser) Mabel Anderson – Nanny to Prince Andrew and Prince Edward, first nanny to Peter Phillips.

Helen Lightbody – Nanny to Prince Charles and Princess Anne.

Barbara Barnes – First nanny to Prince William and Prince Harry.

Alison Wardley – Nanny to Princess Beatrice and Princess Eugenie.

The Duke and Duchess of Gloucester are not on the Civil List and cannot afford to run a full household staff along the lines of senior Royals.

Royals are rarely truly alone, even with other members of the family. There will always be a footman, lady-in-waiting or other member of staff within earshot, if not in the same room.

★ ★

Guests invited to stay at any of the Royal residences are required to hand over undeveloped films from their cameras at the end of a visit. The films are then processed, 'censored' and dispatched to their owners.

★ ★

The Queen spends Easter with her family at Windsor; each branch of the family – the Wales's, the Yorks, the Kents, etc – are housed in separate towers of the castle.

★ ★

At Christmas Prince Philip (head of the family, if not the State), takes all the Royals through their performance during the past year. Official engagements, State occasions, what has been reported in the media – it all comes under the spotlight. Behaviour is a moot point at times, but Prince Philip made his feelings known over the _It's a Royal Knockout_ programme, on which Prince Edward swore at a televised press conference, and the Duchess of York was heard to scream like a fish wife. He was also displeased following Royal Ascot when Diana and her new sister-in-law made headlines every day for a week as a result of their schoolgirl pranks.

★ ★

1988 was the first time the Royal Family celebrated both Christmas and New Year at Sandringham House for a quarter of a century. A major rewiring project at Windsor Castle meant that the Royals could not be accommodated at their usual festive venue. The Royal residences are normally used in rotation – Windsor one year, Sandringham the next – for the celebrations, so that the staff can sometimes spend Christmas with their own families.

HOMES AND GARDENS

Few can conceive of what it must be like to occupy a palace stuffed full of priceless treasures – and how do you make such a place into a home?

Buckingham Palace started its existence as a pleasant but ordinary-looking redbrick building known as Buckingham House. No monarch before Queen Victoria ever used the place as their official residence, preferring St James or Kensington Palace. It was a popular dumping ground, however, for Dowager Queens.

★ ★

The Castle of Mey, Deeside, was virtually derelict when first purchased by the Queen Mother. She said she partly chose the castle because it was a place she hadn't shared with her husband, George VI, and therefore it did not make her quite so sad on visits after she became a widow.

★ ★

The smallest Royal residence: Queen Mary's Doll's House.

The largest Royal residence: Windsor Castle (where visitors can view Queen Mary's Doll's House).

★ ★

Balmoral is a Gaelic word, meaning 'the majestic dwelling'. Queen Victoria preferred to call it 'this dear Paradise'.

What Edward VIII thought of Buckingham Palace:
'It smells.' Said to Walter Monckton (an old university friend and personal legal adviser to the King) during the abdication crisis.

★ ★

The only Royal known to have complained about her rooms at Windsor is Princess Michael of Kent.

★ ★

❝I think it is rather overcrowded. ❞
>—**Prince Andrew,** speaking of the 'Royal Triangle' in Gloucestershire.

★ ★

❝Somewhere close to the M4 would be nice. ❞
>—**Prince Andrew,** in the pre-marriage interview, when asked where he and Sarah wanted to make their permanent home.

AH... IT'S JUST WHAT WE WANTED.

Buckingham Palace was greatly enlarged between 1850 and 1856, at a cost of £150,000. The costs were met by selling the Brighton Pavilion. Up until this time, Queen Victoria's children had been accommodated in the servants' quarters, and guests could not stay overnight.

★ ★

Highgrove House has altered somewhat in appearance since Prince Charles moved there with his new bride in 1981. Classical columns and pediments now adorn the previously plain facade.

★ ★

When Captain Mark Phillips said, 'We're like any other young couple with a mortgage' he wasn't being facetious – he and the Princess Royal at that time held a mortgage for 750 acres of farmland adjoining Gatcombe Park, and for alterations and repairs done to the main house.

★ ★

Who said . . . ?
It's just like camping.
>—**Lady Diana Spencer,** telling friends about her premarriage visits to Highgrove House, to inspect the renovation and decoration.

★ ★

Why has Sunninghill Park, the Duke and Duchess of York's home in Berkshire, caused unfavourable discussion?

1. It has been built on Green Belt land, where planning permission has been denied to others.
2. The job of interior decoration was at first given to an American company, Parish-Hadley.
3. The original design was variously described as 'Southfork' (of *Dallas* fame) or 'Texas ranch-house'. The design was slightly altered.

★ ★

Clearing the lake prior to landscaping the grounds of Sunninghill Park in October 1988, workmen discovered over 100 shells which had lain there since the Second World War.

★ ★

When guests are expected, the Queen inspects their rooms herself.

★ ★

Prince Philip once declared that the Tower of London, of all the Royal residences, had the noisiest plumbing – especially the toilets.

★ ★

The Princess of Wales's bathroom at Kensington Palace is all marble, mirrors and gold-plated fittings . . . just like that of a Hollywood filmstar.

★ ★

Prince Charles collects Victorian hand-painted lavatories and wooden toilet seats.

★ ★

Queen Mary collected jade, Fabergé and miniature items.

★ ★

Princess Michael of Kent collects decorative eggs, in wood, jade, onyx, etc, and displays them on low tables in her Kensington Palace home.

★ ★

To decorate the interior of her first marital home, the Princess Royal chose nineteenth-century wallpapers stored in the attics of Buckingham Palace. All original and in pristine condition, Princess Anne paid for the rolls of wallpaper herself, though the Queen would not have asked for their full value.

★ ★

Three Royal residences with swimming pools:
Buckingham Palace, Highgrove House, Sunninghill Park, home of the Yorks.

It was reputedly the Duke of Edinburgh who vetoed the Duchess of York's plans to have an amusement complex created in the grounds of Sunninghill Park.

★ ★

At Highgrove House, William and Harry have a slide, swings, pet rabbits, their ponies and the swimming pool to keep them amused.

★ ★

The 'covers' (where game is shot) at Sandringham possess quaint names: Folly Hand, Cat's Bottom, Ugly Dale and Wain Hill, to name but a few.

★ ★

Windsor Castle has, a little confusingly, two Home Parks. One is Home Park Public, where the Windsor Horse Show is held. The other is Home Park Private, which is a huge back-yard to the Royals, where Prince Charles exercises furiously on a racing bike.

★ ★

Keen Royal gardeners:
Queen Mary, Queen Elizabeth the Queen Mother, King George VI, Prince Charles.

★ ★

Queen Mary was an 'armchair gardener', assimilating horti-cultural know-how from books and passing her findings on to the army of gardeners employed by the Royal Estates. She would stalk the gardens, poking and prodding the flower beds with her parasol or, later, her stick. She hated ivy with a passion and supervised its removal from the walls of buildings even when she was only there as a guest – her hosts' feelings on the matter were immaterial.

The Queen Mother loves growing old-fashioned roses, hostas, and Himalayan daisies in her garden at the Castle of Mey. She particularly likes sweet pea flowers.

★ ★

The Queen keeps herds of Jersey cattle on her farms, whereas the Queen Mother prefers the shaggy Highland and red-haired Angus breeds. Jersey cattle are renowned for their very rich milk and high-quality cream; Highland and Angus produce the best beef.

★ ★

An attractive feature of the private gardens at Kensington Palace is the rectangular Dutch Pond, around which Royal babies are perambulated to take the air. In spring the pond is flanked by masses of nodding, swaying tulips.

★ ★

One of Prince Charles's favourite herbs is summer savory.

★ ★

Produce grown in the walled kitchen garden of Highgrove House:
Runner beans, carrots, asparagus, tomatoes, lettuce, many varieties of herbs, strawberries, raspberries, blackcurrants.

★ ★

Prince Charles is often happiest when working in the gardens at Highgrove House. The garden on the left front has been carefully managed to become a haven for butterflies and other wildlife. The grasses grow waist high; poppies, corn-flowers and other wild native blooms abound. Under the ground floor windows are well-stocked flower beds – colour, scent and texture are all-important to the Prince and Princess of Wales. To the rear of the house, the Prince decided to mix both decorative and edible plants. A seasonal pergola of runner beans throws shade onto the path, giving way to a huge herb garden. Both gardens and farm land are cultivated organically.

*B*USINESS BEFORE *PLEASURE*

Some Royals run their own business while others have had unusual occupations. They each have their favourite forms of relaxation.

Royal businesses:

The Duke of Edinburgh established a carriage-driving school at Windsor, but it closed in 1989.

Viscount David Linley has an 'heirlooms of the future' shop in the King's Road, Chelsea, selling his furniture designs. He is also in a restaurant partnership with the Earl of Lichfield – they own Deal's, in London's Chelsea Harbour.

The orchards, farms and stud farms at Sandringham are run on a strictly commercial basis.

The Duchy of Cornwall is run on the same lines.

★ ★

For the official opening of Deal's Restaurant, Viscount Linley invited some of London's many drivers of black cabs – thus ensuring that the restaurant was placed well and truly 'on the map'.

★ ★

Princess Michael of Kent has her own interior design company, called Szapar.

Princess Elizabeth wasn't the only female Royal to don uniform in the Second World War. Her cousin, Lady Mary of Gloucester, became a Red Cross nurse.

★ ★

The Duke of Gloucester is a director of British Museum Publications.

★ ★

During the Falklands war, one of Prince Andrew's tasks was to fly decoy for Exocet missiles.

★ ★

Sarah Ferguson's jobs:
An interviewer at Flatmates Unlimited
PR Assistant at Durden-Smith Communications
Nanny, maid and barmaid in Lake Tahoe, USA (without the benefit of the prerequisite Green Card)
PR Assistant to art dealer William Drummond
PR Assistant to the (now defunct) VIP Video Company
Publisher's Assistant at BCK Graphic Arts.

★ ★

The Princess of Wales wanted her friend Sarah Ferguson to be one of her first ladies-in-waiting, but this was vetoed by the Palace because they thought her too inexperienced for the job.

★ ★

Before her marriage, Lady Diana Spencer worked at the Young England Kindergarten in Pimlico, which takes its tiny pupils from the monied, and often titled, classes. There were about fifty children to be supervised, and helped with their art and crafts activities and playtime. Diana chose one of the children, little Clementine Hambro (a great-granddaughter of Sir Winston Churchill), as her bridesmaid.

Unusual occupations for Royalty:

Prince Edward – Production Assistant in a theatre

Princess Alexandra, the Queen's cousin – Auxiliary Nurse

Prince Charles – Cleaning out fly-traps

The Queen (as Princess Elizabeth) – Overhauling engines in HGV army vehicles

Prince William – Cleaning out pet rabbits' hutches

The Queen and other female members of the Royal Family – Selling jams, etc, for the Women's Institute

Princess Anne – Driving a tractor and plough

★ ★

Andrew, Duke of York, is often responsible for the photographic illustration which appears on the Christmas cards sent by the Queen.

★ ★

The Duke of York is also a gifted watercolour artist, as are his older brother and his cousin, Lady Sarah Armstrong-Jones.

★ ★

Who said . . . ?
‘God save the Prince of Wales, and God save us from his architectural judgement. ’
>—Peter Palumbo, Chairman of the Arts Council, on Prince Charles.

★ ★

Books written by Royalty:
The Old Man of Loch Nagar (children's story), *A vision of Britain* – Prince Charles
Crowned in a Far Country – Princess Michael of Kent
Budgie series (children's books) – Duchess of York

Who said . . . ?
❛I'm tone deaf.❜
     —**Prince Philip.** He admits that his singing voice is
       better left unheard.

★ ★

Princess Diana is blessed with perfect pitch.

★ ★

The Queen's second cousin, Tereasa d'Abreu, is a beautiful
and talented rock musician and actress. She is related to the
Queen through the Bowes-Lyon side of the family.

★ ★

Did you know that . . . ?
In 1966, Queen Elizabeth the Queen Mother decided that
London policewomen were looking rather dowdy. Working
with Royal designer Norman Hartnell, she helped come up
with a new style of uniform which included a shorter skirt.

★ ★

The Queen could speak French fluently by the age of ten.

★ ★

❛I find it makes me spit all over the car windows.❜
     —**Diana, Princess of Wales,** to crowds in Wales, who
       asked how her Welsh was progressing.

★ ★

The Princess of Wales is fluent in sign language for the deaf.

★ ★

Unusual Royal amusements:

Prince Charles – Mimicking the Goons

Prince Andrew and Sarah Ferguson – Force-feeding each
other profiteroles in the Royal Box at Ascot

Princess of Wales and Duchess of York – Dressing up as
WPCs

Princess of Wales and Duchess of York, at 1987 Ascot Week – Prodding male bottoms with umbrellas and wolf-whistling at Princess Michael of Kent

The Queen and Princess Margaret – Hiding under tables and giggling during games of Hide and Seek at Christmas

Princess Royal, Prince Edward (he organised the event), *Duke and Duchess of York* – Appearing on television in a celebrity *It's a Knockout*

★ ★

Prince Charles forbade his wife to take part in *It's A Royal Knockout*! Even for charity he would not allow Princess Diana to make a fool of herself in front of the cameras.

★ ★

Royal hobbies:

Princess of Wales – Needlepoint, swimming, all forms of dancing

Duke of York – Photography, designing stamps

★ ★

The Princess of Wales, accompanied by friends from her 'Throne Ranger' circle, regularly visits cinemas in Kensington as a private citizen. They purchase their tickets from the box office – usually back row seats for privacy – after queueing outside with everyone else.

★ ★

Forms of Royal relaxation:

Prince Charles – Listening to cello music, meditating

The Queen Mother – Listening to the specially installed 'bookie's blower' in Clarence House

DISTINGUISHING FEATURES AND FOIBLES

They can be rude, vulgar, caring, courageous and bad-tempered . . . like the rest of us, the Royals are only human!

Who said . . . ?
‹I'm so tall and so blonde, no one can help noticing me when I enter a room.›

—**Princess Michael of Kent.**

★ ★

When Royals have cried:
The Duke of Windsor, at his wedding to Mrs Simpson. (She remained dry-eyed throughout.)

Prince Charles, at the funeral of Lord Louis Mountbatten.

Sarah, Duchess of York, after meeting an orphaned child survivor of the Zeebrugge Ferry disaster. She bought him a large toy truck as she had promised.

The Princess of Wales when she made a special detour to receive flowers from a schoolgirl whose mother had promised to take her to the 'walkabout', but who died of cancer before the visit.

Queen Mary, at the wedding of Princess Elizabeth to the Duke of Edinburgh.

Prince Edward has an even more spectacular bald patch than his brother Charles.

Royal experts at the art of swearing:

Duke of Edinburgh – At pressmen who harass him at airports.

Princess Royal – At pressmen who ask what she considers to be impertinent or irrelevant questions.

Prince Edward – At pressmen, following the _It's a Royal Knockout_ programme. They weren't happy with the meagre coverage they had been given; he thought they should be grateful.

★ ★

Two young Royals who have poked their tongues out at the press:

Zara Phillips – During the Tidworth Gymkhana in Hampshire, in which she was a competitor.

Prince Harry – Arriving at kindergarten. He was in the rear of the car, and received a reprimand from Princess Diana.

The best behaved Royal children:
Lord Frederick Windsor and his sister Lady Gabriella, son and daughter of Prince and Princess Michael of Kent.

★ ★

What Queen Mary used to do to George V:
She would prod his bottom with the point of her umbrella and say, 'Now, George,' if she thought his speech had gone on long enough, or if he swore in public.

★ ★

Words of courage . . .
'Let us go forward . . . as one man, a smile on our lips, and our heads held high, and with God's help we will not fail. '
> —**George VI,** broadcasting to the nation, 24 May 1940.

★ ★

Of whom was it said . . . ?
'She always looks right at you. '
> —**The Queen Mother.**

★ ★

'She's like an old-fashioned rose, not brightly coloured but very fragrant. '
> —**The Queen Mother,** by Anne Morrow Lindbergh.

★ ★

As an undergraduate at Trinity College, Cambridge, Prince Charles would shop and cook for himself – when the Queen arrived on private visits to her son, he would cook for both of them. When going home he would travel down to London on the regular rail service and on one occasion, when there was standing room only, he gave his first class ticket to an elderly woman so that she could sit in his compartment. He, in turn, took her second class ticket and stood for the rest of the journey.

Anne Boleyn, ill-fated second wife of Henry VIII, had six fingers on each hand.

George VI's stutter plagued him from his school days onwards, condemning him to a life of miserable public speaking.

★ ★

Of whom was it said . . . ?
'He . . . gives a convincing impression of sinking into . . . premature, cerebral middle age.'
> —**Prince Charles,** by Ingrid Seward, Editor of *Majesty* magazine.

★ ★

Of whom was it said . . . ?
'He never lets you forget who his mother is.'
> —**Duke of York,** by a fellow crew member on HMS *Invincible*.

*F*AVOURITE AND NOT SO FAVOURITE THINGS

Just like everyone else, each of the Royals has their own likes and dislikes. Some are more surprising than others.

The Queen and Queen Mother both enjoy *Coronation Street* (no pun intended!) and the BBC Radio 4 serial *The Archers*.

★　★

The Queen, the Queen Mother and Princess Diana are all fans of the Australian soap opera *Neighbours.*

★　★

Princess Diana is a fan of Miss Piggy and Kermit from *The Muppets*, and the *Peanuts* cartoon strip, especially Snoopy.

★　★

Princess Diana's favourite film of 1989 was the Oscar-winning *Rainman* starring Dustin Hoffman. Autism is one of the Princess's concerns.

★　★

The Queen Mother loves the songs of Elizabeth Welch and Noel Coward.

★　★

The Queen enjoys listening to jazz, Frank Sinatra, Perry Como and Barbra Streisand.

Prince Charles listens to opera recordings on compact disc.

★ ★

Princess Diana likes David Bowie, Michael Jackson, Dire Straits, Supertramp and Janet Jackson.

★ ★

Princess Diana's favourite classical composers: Rachmaninov, Tchaikovsky, Brahms, Dvořák.

★ ★

Which musical made the Duchess of York cry? *The Phantom of the Opera*, which she has seen four times.

★ ★

The Duchess of York's favourite singer is Chris de Burgh. She and the Duke played 'Lady in Red' constantly during their honeymoon cruise.

★ ★

Princess Michael likes the music of David Bowie.

★ ★

Favourite Royal reading matter:

Princess of Wales – Novels by Danielle Steele, Judith Krantz and Jeffrey Archer

Prince of Wales – Freudian tracts, and books on religion, Lord Mountbatten, philosophy

The Queen – Books on dog breeding and bloodstock lines

The Queen Mother – *Sporting Life*

★ ★

Prince Philip enjoys books about the sea, sailing, photography and sport. A large proportion of his free time is also taken up with reading books and journals on science, industry and conservation.

The Princess Royal would rather be out and about than lounging in front of the television or reading a book. When she does read, she often chooses books on sport, horses, travel and dogs.

★　★

Princess Margaret and Prince Edward share a love of anything theatrical. Books about theatre and theatre craft, biographies of actors and actresses, librettos, all make pleasurable reading matter for these two Royals.

★　★

Prince Philip enjoys gin and tonic, champagne and real ale – not all at the same time, of course!

★　★

Andrew, Duke of York, rarely drinks anything except ginger beer at parties and official engagements, though he does like champagne.

★　★

The Queen Mother likes English 'bitter' beer.

★　★

Royals who have enjoyed tobacco:
Edward VII, George V, George VI, Duke of Windsor, Princess Margaret (though she now uses a cigarette holder).

Those who have hated tobacco:
Prince Albert, Queen Victoria, Princess Diana.

And those who have kicked the habit:
Duke of Edinburgh, the Honourable Angus Ogilvy, Sarah, Duchess of York.

★　★

What the Queen dislikes:
People who are pompous snobs; being touched too familiarly by official guides on tour; not being kept informed by the government of the day; being bored.

What the Queen does like:
Horse-racing – especially The Classics; knowledgeable conversation concerning horses and dogs; riding or walking alone on the moors at Balmoral; family weddings and baptisms; personally choosing Christmas and birthday gifts.

★ ★

The Princess of Wales hates the pomp and formality of life at Court. The Duchess of York loves it.

★ ★

Who said . . . ?
❝I hate all that heel-clicking and bowing. ❞
　　　　　　　　　　　　—Diana, Princess of Wales.

★ ★

The Queen dislikes helicopter travel. The Queen Mother loves it.

★ ★

The Queen Mother enjoys watching a good football or rugby match.

★ ★

The Duchess of Windsor didn't care much for children of any age, but positively disliked small babies.

★ ★

Three things which frightened Queen Mary:
Thunderstorms; gunfire of any kind, including Royal salutes; the sight of blood.

★ ★

The Duchess of York is terrified of snakes.

★ ★

One of George V's favourite words: *'Bugger!'*
. . . and his most famous comment: *'Bugger Bognor!'*

DUTY CALLS

'**W**ork is the rent you pay for the position you occupy on Earth,' the Queen Mother once told her eldest daughter. This section includes just a tiny proportion of the total engagements undertaken by the Royals.

Princess Elizabeth's first solo public engagement took place on 30 November 1944, when she launched HMS *Vanguard*. Three years later, she sailed with her parents and sister on this ship to South Africa.

★ ★

Princess Elizabeth received the Freedom of the City of Edinburgh on 16 July 1947. On this occasion she was accompanied by her fiancé.

★ ★

The first time Princess Elizabeth attended the State Opening of Parliament was 21 October 1947.

★ ★

At military parades, when the Queen (or any other Royal) inspects the ranks of assembled servicemen and women, none of them is supposed to look the monarch or her representative straight in the eye – even if she stops to speak to them.

★ ★

When blank cartridges were fired at the Queen as she rode in a Trooping the Colour procession in June 1988, it was not the first time such a thing had happened. In 1936, the still uncrowned Edward VIII was riding to the ceremony at which he would present Colours to the Guards Regiments, when a loaded revolver landed at his horse's feet; a man was arrested for this incident, while Edward VIII rode on without turning a hair.

Prince Philip made his first public speech, as Lieutenant Philip Mountbatten, at Corsham, Wiltshire, on 1 November 1947.

★ ★

Who said . . . ?
'If you stay here too long, you'll develop slitty eyes.'
　　—**Duke of Edinburgh,** to a group of Western students during the Queen's visit to China in 1986.

★ ★

On St David's Day (1 March) 1990, the Queen and Prince Philip went to Purbright Camp, Surrey, to present leeks to the Welsh Guardsmen.

★ ★

Countries visited by the Queen and Prince Philip in 1989 and early 1990:

Japan	Prince Philip for the funeral of Emperor Hirohito – February 1989.
Barbados	Joint visit – March 1989.
Channel Islands	Both visited for three days – May 1989.
Canada	Joint visit – 27 June to 1 July 1989.
Singapore	Joint visit – 9 to 11 October 1989.
Malaysia	Joint visit – 14 to 17 October 1989.
New Zealand	Joint visit – February 1990.

Who said . . . ?
‹I didn't stop to ask them if they knew who I was. ›
> —**Princess Royal,** on a Save the Children Fund trip to
> Africa in 1985.

★ ★

‹You don't have to like children to want to help them. ›
> —**Princess Royal,** in the Walden Interview on
> Independent Television, 11 December 1988.

★ ★

On 3 March 1990, the Princess Royal fulfilled one of her
typically punishing schedules:
She first visited the City of Sheffield. As Patron of Uni-
versiade '91, she attended the World Student Games'
Topping Off celebrations. After lunch, the Princess Royal
declared the Age Concern Centre officially open. There followed a call on the YMCA, then the charity shops of the Save
the Children Fund.

★ ★

The first speech to be both written and delivered by the
Princess of Wales:
On 18 October 1988, at the annual Dr Barnardo's conference,
the Princess spoke of the charity's work, and her fears for
children growing up with drink, drugs, violence and prosti-
tution. She also raised the subject of single-parent families
and the need for a stable, loving family life.

★ ★

On 14 December 1988, Princess Diana sat in on a meeting
between a married couple and their counsellor at the Wol-
verhampton branch of Relate, the UK marriage guidance
service.

★ ★

On National No Smoking Day (8 March 1989), Princess Diana marked the occasion by visiting patients suffering from chest complaints in Bart's Hospital, London.

★ ★

The Princess of Wales rarely wears gloves on a walkabout, no matter what the weather. This is because so many women want to admire her engagement ring.

★ ★

‹*It sits like a pea on a drum.***›**
> —**Prince Charles,** during the 1985 tour of Australia, when he and the Princess of Wales had to don protective headgear for a factory tour.

★ ★

Who said . . . ?
‹*I'll see* **you** *later!***›**
> —**The Duchess of York,** in answer to good-natured heckling from a parliamentarian during the Yorks' tour of North America in 1987.

★ ★

When the Duchess of York visited survivors of the December 1988 Clapham Junction rail disaster in hospital, she discovered that two of the injured were personal friends. She also said that, prior to her marriage, she had often travelled to London on that particular train.

★ ★

At the official opening of the Mount Annan Botanical Gardens in Sydney, Australia, in August 1988, the Duke and Duchess of York were planting a Lilly Pilly tree to commemorate the event, when a sudden gust of wind across the open hillside revealed rather more of Fergie's upper thigh than is usually seen in public.

Last TV appearance of the Duke of York in 1988:
He travelled direct to Lockerbie in Scotland to view the wreckage of the Pan-Am jumbo jet, and to comfort the survivors of the air disaster. Dressed in Royal Naval working dress, the Duke was visibly distressed as he spoke to reporters.

★　★

The redoubtable Queen Mary had two tried and trusted tips for those new to the Royal 'firm': during public engagements, one should sit down whenever possible, and avail oneself of toilet facilities whenever the opportunity arose. This guidance was, in turn, passed on to Princess Diana and the Duchess of York.

★　★

The Palace of Westminster (Houses of Parliament) is the property of the reigning monarch – it is merely loaned to Parliament. Each year it is 'prorogued', and then 'returned' to Parliament for its use, at the State Opening ceremony.

★　★

The Trooping the Colour ceremony takes place in the Tilting Yard, so-called because such kings as Henry VIII enjoyed watching jousting tournaments there.

★　★

‹Your War of Independence means you can just shake hands. ›
> —A British diplomat, outlining Royal protocol and etiquette to Americans prior to the Princess of Wales's visit to New York in February 1989.

★　★

Princess Alexandra opened the sixty-sixth Ideal Home Exhibition in 1989 and was introduced to a man who could build a house in just a fortnight.

The Duke of Gloucester was present in Belfast on 21 February 1989, for the memorial service held in St Anne's Cathedral to remember the dead in the Midlands–M1 air disaster.

★ ★

The memorial service for those killed in the 1988 Lockerbie–Pan Am disaster was attended by, amongst others, Margaret Thatcher, Neil Kinnock and the US Ambassador but no members of the Royal Family. While it is quite normal for the Queen to send a representative to such occasions, it is not unknown for her to attend in person – Aberfan, for example. That apart, one of the Royals holidaying at Balmoral could have gone in their own right. It is a major blot on the Royals' copybook that will not be erased for some time.

★ ★

Who said . . . ?
'I'd go anywhere for a free meal.'
—Princess Michael of Kent.

I COULD HAVE SWORN THAT LAST ONE LOOKED LIKE PRINCESS MICHAEL OF KENT

Some Royal patronages:

The Queen Mother – Friends of St Paul's Cathedral, Friends of St Martin-in-the-Fields, The Royal Hospital and Home, Putney, The Royal College of Obstetricians and Gynaecologists.

The Queen – Battersea Dogs Home, Queen's Award for Export and Technology, Women's Institute, Queen's Award for Industry.

Duke of Edinburgh – World Wildlife Fund (or Worldwide Fund for Nature), Duke of Edinburgh's Award, Prince Philip Cup for Pony Club Teams, Prince Philip Awards to Royal Association of British Dairy Farmers.

Princess Margaret – National Society for the Prevention of Cruelty to Children, Royal Scottish Society for the Prevention of Cruelty to Children.

The Prince of Wales – Prince's Trust, Asian Affairs Society, United World Colleges, Business in the Community, Prince of Wales Awards for Industrial Innovation.

The Princess of Wales – British Lung Foundation, Help the Aged, Birthright, Crusaid, British Red Cross, Welsh National Opera, Turning Point, Pre-Schools Playgroups Association.

The Princess Royal – Riding For The Disabled, Save the Children Fund, British Knitting and Clothing Export Council, Royal Lymington Yacht Club.

Duchess of York – Leukaemia Research Fund, The Samaritans, Association of Flower Arrangement Societies.

Duke of York – Aycliffe Special School, County Durham.

ROVING ROYALS

The Queen has fabulous cars and fairytale coaches yet her favourite mode of transport is on horseback. Prince Charles treasures his Aston Martin, while his wife drives a homely Ford Escort. What other modes of transport do Royals use? And where do they go in them?

The present-day Royal barge is named the *Royal Nore* (as was the previous one), but it is no longer used for transporting those guilty of treason to the Tower of London . . .

★ ★

The passenger cabins on helicopters of the Queen's Flight are sound-proofed, so conversations remain private.

★ ★

Royal pilots:
George VI, Duke of Edinburgh, Prince of Wales, Andrew, Duke of York, Sarah, Duchess of York. George, Duke of Kent and William, brother of the present Duke of Gloucester, were also qualified pilots; both died young, in plane crashes.

★ ★

When making private visits to his parents at the Royal residences, the Duke of York has been known to land his helicopter on the lawns outside.

★ ★

Of whom was it said . . . ?

'She is a very good and extremely careful and considerate driver. '

— **Princess Elizabeth,** by her Company Commander at the Number 1 MTT Centre, Camberley, 1945.

★　★

The Royal Yacht *Britannia* has a wine cellar, cinema facilities, a garage for a Rolls Royce, and a State Staircase. It carries a full stock of dark blue cotton shirts and trousers, in all sizes, and blankets, for shipwreck or evacuation victims. It can be quickly converted to a hospital ship – its wartime role – and saw action in the Falklands War. The Royal Yacht carries no armaments of any kind. It picked up British nationals evacuated from Yemen during the civil disturbances there in 1987, and even turned back at one point to pick up a late arrival at the beach. It is crewed by regular members of the Royal Navy, who apply or are selected for Special Duties.

★　★

Cars driven by the Royal Family:

Duke of Edinburgh, the Queen, Captain Mark Phillips – Range Rover

Prince Charles – Aston Martin

Princess Margaret – Rolls Royce

Princess of Wales, Lady Sarah Armstrong-Jones – Mini

Princess of Wales – Ford Escort

Duchess of York – Jaguar sports car (she used to drive a Mercedes Benz but had to switch to a British make on her marriage).

★　★

Members of the Royal Family who have committed driving offences: Captain Mark Phillips, Viscount Linley.

Royals who have been involved in car accidents:
Lord Snowdon (when still married to Princess Margaret), Captain Mark Phillips, Prince Philip (in a black MG sports car much liked by his wife), Prince Charles (in his beloved Aston Martin, only days after telling Princess Diana to 'Get off the bonnet before you dent it!').

★ ★

Marion Crawford, governess to Princess Elizabeth and Princess Margaret Rose, took her two young charges for their first ride on the Underground in London. All went well until somebody recognised them, then they had to retreat to the Station Master's office, where Miss Crawford summoned a Royal car to come and rescue them.

★ ★

How Prince and Princess Michael of Kent celebrated their tenth wedding anniversary:
They travelled on the Orient Express back to Vienna, where they had married on 30 June 1978.

★ ★

Unlikely Royal modes of transport:
Miniature Aston Martin – Presented to Prince Andrew when he was a small child.

Horse-drawn cart with two wicker chairs in the back – Used in the war years to transport Queen Mary round the Badminton estate.

The footplate of a New Zealand steam locomotive – George VI.

A large motorbike – Used by the Duke of Gloucester 'for dodging around London'.

Pale blue beach buggy – In which Lady Diana Spencer learned to drive on the Althorp estate.

★ ★

In 1959, the Queen Mother paid an official visit to Kenya. Despite political unrest at the time, the trip was a great success – especially with the Masai tribesmen. The land was suffering a drought, and the Queen Mother sympathetically voiced her hope that they would be 'blessed with rain'. Within 30 minutes of her speech, there was an almighty thunderstorm. The Masai decided that she must be a goddess, at least.

★ ★

When the Queen and Prince Philip visited the Arab countries in November 1986, a precedent was set: the Queen was created an 'Honorary Gentleman', so that she could attend otherwise all-male banquets and functions. The Saudi King also presented her with a special gift – a solid gold handbag. It has yet to be seen on state occasions.

On her first visit to Australia as Princess of Wales in March 1983, Diana was struck in the eye by a bouquet, thrown by an enthusiastic member of the crowd.

The highly acclaimed BBC Television children's programme *Blue Peter* received a Royal seal of approval in the seventies when one of the presenters, Valerie Singleton, was invited to join Princess Anne on a trip to the Treetops Hotel in Kenya. Together they watched and photographed the wildlife, and waged a joint struggle when it came to keeping curious monkeys off the balcony where meals were served.

★   ★

The Duke of York is the only Royal to have visited the Falkland Islands.

★   ★

‘If we take her, everyone will say she's too young to travel; if we don't, they'll say we're being cruel. ’
> —**The Duke of York,** when asked whether Princess Beatrice would accompany her parents to Australia in 1988.

★   ★

The Duchess of York had her first skiing holiday of 1989 in January. She went to Klosters, where Major Hugh Lindsay was killed in an avalanche in 1988. She was accompanied by her husband.

★   ★

Favourite holiday spots:

George V – Sandringham, Norfolk

Princess Margaret – 'Les Jolies Eaux', Mustique

Prince Charles – Vopnasfiord, Iceland

Prince William and Prince Harry – Majorca, Spain

The Queen – Balmoral, Scotland

The Queen Mother – Castle of Mey, Deeside

Princess Michael of Kent – Club St James, Caribbean.

GOOD SPORTS

On land, at sea and in the air, Royal sportsmen and women have excelled themselves in a great variety of sports, from scuba-diving to horse-riding, from tennis to fishing.

Royals who have competed in the Olympic Games:
Princess Anne, Captain Mark Phillips, King Olav of Norway, King Juan Carlos of Spain, Prince Albert of Monaco.

★ ★

Which Royal presented an Olympic medal to another?
The Princess Royal to her husband, Mark Phillips, at the Seoul Olympic Games, 1988.

★ ★

George VI played cricket, football, squash and golf. He also loved swimming and was an excellent horse-rider who hunted regularly. But he really excelled at tennis. Before he became King, he won the Mixed Doubles Competition at the Highgate Tennis Club, partnered by Miss Peggy Bouverie, in 1919. He followed this up the next year by becoming Men's Doubles Champion of the RAF with his great friend Wing-Commander Louis Greig. Together, they entered for the Men's Doubles at Wimbledon in 1926 but were beaten, after a hard-fought match, by two former champions, Barrett and Gore. Always modest, the then Duke of York refused an invitation to play this opening round on Centre Court. 'I'm not a champion yet,' he said.

The Duke of Edinburgh is Patron of the Cornwall Rugby Football Union.

★ ★

Four dangerous sports pursued by the Prince of Wales:
Parachuting, polo, scuba-diving on submerged wrecks, skiing on glaciers and in avalanche areas.

★ ★

Three not so dangerous sports enjoyed by the Prince of Wales:
Salmon fishing, swimming, windsurfing.

★ ★

In 1976, Great Britain suffered one of the worst droughts in its history. Reservoirs, lakes and rivers dried up, but Prince Charles managed to catch seven salmon in a single day on the River Dee.

★ ★

On the second part of their honeymoon, Prince Charles showed his bride how to fly-fish for salmon on the same stretch of the River Dee where he had been taught the art by his grandmother.

★ ★

The Princess of Wales enjoys watching Sumo wrestling on television.

★ ★

At the 1988 Boat Show in London, one of the most famous visitors to Earl's Court was the Princess Royal. An expert sailor herself (taught by her father), the Princess requested details of family-size dinghies.

★ ★

Four sports at which the Duchess of York excels:
Swimming, netball (she was Captain of her school team), skiing (she is a Black Run skier), horse-riding.

Andrew, Duke of York, is a life member of the Mountbatten Sports Complex in Plymouth.

★ ★

Prince Edward and the Duke of York both played rugby football at school.

★ ★

Prince Edward shares with his Tudor ancestors a love of Real Tennis, which is still played at Hampton Court. Royal exponents of the game include Henry VIII and Elizabeth I.

★ ★

Which Royal ran in the 1987 London Marathon?
Marina Ogilvy.

★ ★

One of the Queen's most enduring ambitions is to own a Derby-winning racehorse.

★ ★

The Queen does not approve of the British fashion of translating jockey's silk racing colours into sweatshirts. Her mother doesn't mind at all.

★ ★

De rigueur clothing for Royals attending horse shows comprises green wellies, Barbour or tweed jackets, tweed or corduroy flat caps and, for the Queen, a Hermès headscarf. These outfits are reproduced in miniature for the Royal tots, naturally.

★ ★

Who said . . . ?
❬I think we went a little too far today, David. ❭
        —**George V** to the Prince of Wales, after a shoot at
        Sandringham which culminated in a bag of 4,000
        pheasants.

Prince Charles's racehorse trainer, Mr Nick Gaselee, was fined £2,000 by the Jockey Club following the discovery that the Prince's horse, Devil's Elbow, won a race in December 1988, under the influence of a prohibited substance accidentally administered. The 'dope' was, in fact, a tonic prescribed by a vet. Mr Gaselee apologised for any embarrassment caused to Prince Charles. The prize money had to be returned.

★ ★

On the polo ground, Prince Charles will strip off his shirt and down a pint of beer in full view of everyone.

★ ★

Who said . . . ?
'It's good practice for parachute jumping. '
 —**Prince Charles,** on the sport of three-day eventing.

HORSE AND HOUND

Dogs and horses seem to play an important role in the lives of the Royal Family. Can you imagine the Queen without her Corgis? Or Charles without his polo ponies? Unthinkable!

As a child, the Queen Mother had a pet bullfinch named Bobby and a Shetland pony called Bobs.

★　★

The Queen received her first riding lessons on a Shetland pony named Peggy, and was taught by her father's groom, Owen.

★　★

The Queen's drum horses, which have appeared in so many ceremonial processions, are named Coriolanus and Caractacus. The horses *do* wear special inserts in their ears, to prevent their hearing being damaged by the loud drums.

★　★

After the Trooping the Colour ceremony and other parades, the Queen visits her horses in the Royal Mews to feed them fresh carrots.

★　★

Prince Charles takes a jar of sugar lumps with him for the ponies when he goes to play polo.

The Princess Royal's first pony was called Greensleeves. Her mother taught her to ride at the age of two and a half.

★ ★

At the 1971 Badminton Horse Trials, two years before his marriage to her daughter, Captain Mark Phillips received his prize from the Queen – a show-jumping saddle.

★ ★

The Princess Royal and the Duchess of York both rode Aldaniti, to raise money for the Bob Champion Cancer Trust.

★ ★

Of whom was it said . . . ?
'What she doesn't know isn't worth knowing. '
>—A close friend of the Royal Family, on the Queen's knowledge of horses and dogs.

★ ★

Corgis are a registered breed of Welsh sheepdog.

★ ★

Unless unavoidably detained elsewhere, the Queen always feeds her dogs herself, in her study, mixing each bowlful to the pet's individual taste.

★ ★

The Queen was accompanied on her honeymoon by her pet Corgi, Crackers (not Susan, as is usually reported).

★ ★

Who said . . . ?
'There are always lots of Corgis about, snapping at one's ankles. '
>—**Princess Michael of Kent,** when asked by Terry Wogan, on his TV chat show, what it was like at Buckingham Palace.

★ ★

The favourite dogs of the Earl and Countess of Strathmore, grandparents of the Queen, were Chows. As a baby, the Queen loved to play with them.

★ ★

George VI's favourite dogs were Labradors, and at the time of his Accession he kept three of the golden variety – Mimsey, plus two of her puppies, Scrummy (a bitch) and Stiffy, (a dog). Choo-choo was a 'hairy-coated animal', and the two little Princesses had a Corgi each, Jane and Dookie.

★ ★

Some of the Duke and Duchess of Windsor's pet dogs: Slipper (also called Slippy Poo or Mr Loo), Disraeli, Trooper, Imp, Davy Crockett, Preezie. They referred to the dogs as 'our babies'.

★ ★

Princess Diana insists that her husband's black Labrador, Harvey, has a kennel outside. She cannot bear large dogs in the house, and does not forgive canine 'accidents' on floors and furniture.

★ ★

Prince Andrew gave his wife a dog which they named Bendicks – after the Queen's favourite brand of chocolate. Buckingham Palace, in answer to enquiries, said it was a 'Warwickshire Terrier'. In fact no such breed exist. The dog resembles a cross between a Jack Russell and a Sealyham.

★ ★

Princess Margaret has a 'Dawgie' – a cross between a Corgi belonging to the Queen, and the Corgi's Dachshund lover.

★ ★

Princess Anne has a Labrador named Moriarty (a present from Prince Charles) and a 'very laid back' Bloodhound.

Royal certainties:

While the Queen and her family are well-known for their bloodstock interests, the Royal connection with greyhound racing has been less publicised. Prince Philip owned a dog named Camira Flash, which won the 1968 Greyhound Derby at White City. Although it has been some years since the Prince owned a greyhound, others – notably Playfield Leader and Prince Rupert – have raced under his name; winnings go to one of Prince Philip's charities, the National Playing Fields Association.

Hardy King, another winning dog, races on behalf of the Princess Royal. Again, any prize money goes to charity – in this case the Save the Children Fund. Princess Diana, wearing bow tie, dashing dinner jacket and evening trousers, has presented trophies at the Wembley Stadium dog track – and picked up winnings herself.

PLEASING THE ROYAL PALATE

Surprisingly the Royals have quite simple tastes where food and drink are concerned. Find out how to cook the Queens favourite dessert, or mix a cocktail for Princess Margaret and the Duchess of York.

At State banquets and other formal dinners, Royal chefs carefully bone meat and fillet fish, so that guests don't have to worry about 'difficult' dishes, which would also upset the delicate timetable of such meals.

★ ★

Seafood is *never* eaten by Royals on official engagements, but they do eat it at home.

★ ★

Prince Charles will eat anything that is put in front of him, but when the Queen is on an official engagement or State Visit, a list of 'forbidden' foods is sent ahead.

★ ★

The Royal Family eat eggs only from free-range hens.

★ ★

Queen Victoria adored chocolate ice-cream. It was one thing which, despite the entreaties of her doctors as her age and girth advanced, she absolutely refused to give up.

Favourite Royal titbits:

The Queen – Bendicks superfine chocolate

Prince Charles – Dessert apples

Princess of Wales – Chocolate Bath Oliver biscuits

Princes Harry and William – Fresh strawberries

★ ★

Deal's, the London restaurant co-owned by Viscount Linley and the Earl of Lichfield, specialises in sushi, hamburgers and spare ribs.

★ ★

What to expect when at tea with the Queen:
Bread and butter, pâtés, fish pastes, cucumber sandwiches, biscuits, rich chocolate cake, chocolate wafer biscuits, potted shrimps, and lots of tea, which Her Majesty brews herself from the little table beside her.

★ ★

The Queen Mother's tea table:
In true Scottish fashion, the Queen Mother plies her teatime guests with plenty of delicious food:
Scones (plain, potato and fruit), black bun, rich chocolate cake, teabreads, shortbread, smoked salmon sandwiches.

★ ★

The Queen enjoys lamb cutlets, preferably served with fresh mint sauce, well-done steaks, and curry.

★ ★

One of the Queen's favourite desserts is Banana Caramel, preferably with extra sauce.

★ ★

Prince Philip always has a cooked breakfast, and loves potted shrimps for tea.

A typical 'at home' dinner for the Queen and Prince Philip:

Vegetable Consommé

Trout Grilled with Lemon and Herbs
New Potatoes
Green Salad

Vanilla Ice-cream with Caramel Sauce

Cheese or a Savoury, such as Anchovy Toast

★ ★

The first course served at Princess Anne's Wedding Breakfast
was scrambled eggs with smoked salmon.

★ ★

Which member of the Royal Family has been an avid follower
of Weight Watchers?
The Queen.

★ ★

Who said . . . ?
❛I do not diet. I do not have a problem. ❜
    —**Sarah Ferguson,** in her pre-wedding interview.

The Princess Royal's slim figure belies her sweet tooth.

★ ★

Green's in Mayfair is one of Princess Margaret's favourite restaurants.

★ ★

Princess Diana's favourite confectionery:
Bubble gum, strawberry chewits, Cadbury's Roses, Yorkie bars, fudge, Mars Bars.

★ ★

Princess Diana loves cream of watercress soup, gravlax, fromage frais, ice-cream and sorbet.

★ ★

Favourite London restaurants of the Princess of Wales:
San Lorenzo, Pot au Feu, Topolino, Green's (Prince William likes the salmon fishcakes).

★ ★

Princess Diana hates chips (or French Fries), as does Prince Charles.

★ ★

The Prince and Princess of Wales are *not* vegetarians, but they do not like steak, and would rather eat chicken or fish.

★ ★

Princess Diana and Prince Charles both eat lots of yoghurt, often in place of high-calorie desserts.

★ ★

In honour of a Prince:
The dessert *Sorbet aux Fruits Prince Guillaume* was created in honour of Prince Charles's eldest son.

Who said . . . ?

'I'd walk a mile for a bacon sandwich. '
> —**Princess Diana,** to a group of workmen on a project she was visiting with Prince Charles.

★ ★

'I bet your breakfast will be better than anything we'll get in there. '
> —**Prince Charles,** to the same group of workmen.

★ ★

'I often pop into Sainsbury's to buy the boys' tea. '
> —**The Princess of Wales,** on opening a rival super-market.

★ ★

The Duke of York eats in the same Mess, and partakes of identical meals, as the rest of his Navy colleagues. 'Post op fry-ups' are still usual for those returning from flying sorties – eggs, bacon, tomatoes, mushrooms, toast and coffee, which the Duke drinks from a plain white mug. He walks up to the dining room hatch with everyone else to queue for his meals.

★ ★

The Duchess of York has introduced the Queen Mother to the delights of Chinese food, and they accompany one another to Fergie's favourite Chinese restaurant in the King's Road, London. Fergie's favourite dish is oysters in ginger sauce. For dessert, the Queen Mother has a bowl of chilled lychees.

★ ★

Favourite London restaurants of the Duchess of York:
The upstairs restaurant of Harvey Nichols, Carlton Tower Hotel (now Hyatt Carlton Tower), Basil Street Hotel's Parrot Club, the Salad Bar of Upstairs Downstairs (the Salad Bar is downstairs).

★ ★

Princess Michael of Kent stated on television that her favourite meal was egg, chips (or French fries) and baked beans, which her children also enjoy.

Prince Edward hates caviar.

★　★

Who said . . . ?
'After all those cocktails, it's just another drink. '
　　—**The Duchess of Windsor,** explaining why soup was
　　rarely served at her dinner parties.

★　★

Champagne cocktails are served at Royal Christmas parties.
Soft drinks are available for non-alcohol drinkers, drivers and
pregnant women.

★　★

One of Princess Margaret's favourite cocktails is a
Margharita.

★　★

The Queen Mother likes Dubonnet – with gin in it.

★　★

Anne, the Princess Royal, drinks Diet Coca-Cola.

★　★

The Princess of Wales drinks decaffeinated coffee at home;
and she doesn't mind drinking it from a paper cup if
necessary.

★　★

Prince Charles does not care much for hot drinks. His ideal
refreshing drink is a glass of warm water with a fresh lemon
squeezed into it.

★　★

Non-alcoholic cocktails invented for Fergie and Andrew's
wedding:
Fergie's Fancy, Bands of Gold, Wedded Bliss, Windsor
Sunrise, Purple Velvet, Buckingham Fizz, Hello, Sailor!

DESIGNER ROYALS

Which Royals prefer what colours? How much do the Princess of Wales and Duchess of York pay for their shoes? And why does the Princess Royal believe in wearing the same clothes several times?

Favourite items of clothing worn by the Royals:

The Princess of Wales – A sweater depicting a koala bear on the front, and a map of Australia on the back.

The Queen – A silver brocade evening dress designed by Norman Hartnell.

The Queen Mother – Flowery chiffon dresses and 'Paddington Bear' hats.

The Duchess of York – Ski suits.

★   ★

Favourite colours:

The Queen – Most pastel shades. White is usually reserved for the dresses she wears on State occasions.

The Queen Mother – Turquoise, bright blue and bright pink.

The Duchess of York – Bottle green, maroon; black for gala evening wear.

The Princess of Wales – Bright scarlet, beige, dove grey, pale blue and bright, arty prints.

Lindka Ceirach is the favoured designer of the Duchess of York, Duchess of Kent, Duchess of Westminster and the Queen of Greece.

★ ★

Royals who dye their hair:
The Princess of Wales: 'Charles prefers blondes.'
The Queen: a shade called 'Chocolate Kiss' is used.

★ ★

The Duchess of Kent's hairdresser is Michael at Michaeljohn.

★ ★

Princess Diana prefers the pochette, or clutch bag, while the Princess Royal and the Duchess of York favour shoulder bags. Queen Victoria owned a handbag with a poodle embroidered on it.

★ ★

Lady Sarah Armstrong-Jones wears Swatch watches.

★ ★

❛*I always wear my best clothes when visiting friends!*❜
      —**The Queen Mother,** rebuffing a courtier who had suggested that she wear something 'more suitable' when visiting Blitz victims in the East End of London.

★ ★

On her arrival in China in 1986, the Queen wore a yellow silk suit – a suitable choice, as yellow is regarded as the luckiest colour by the Chinese – and it wasn't chosen by accident.

★ ★

Prince Philip never wears anything in bed. (He didn't even take a pair of pyjamas on his honeymoon.)

The Queen Mother has rarely been seen without her pearl necklace . . . even when she went fishing for salmon in the River Dee.

Did you know that . . .

George V wore 'combination' underwear made from pure English wool, with the necessary button-flap in the rear? Queen Mary chose them for him.

★　★

Who said . . . ?

Good God, what are you wearing? It looks like a bathmat!
— **Prince Charles,** on meeting his brother Edward in New Zealand. Edward was wearing a Maori cloak of kiwi feathers.

★　★

Prince Charles thinks silk boxer shorts are 'The sexiest underwear I've ever seen.'

★　★

Princess Diana received two black satin *Thriller* bomber jackets from Michael Jackson, for Princes William and Harry.

★ ★

Clothes designers favoured by Prince William and Prince Harry:
Osh Kosh, Yves St Laurent, Benetton 0–12, Pierre Cardin. Chainstores: Mothercare and BhS; footwear from 'Rayne Drops'.

★ ★

Who said . . . ?
'Why buy something new when there is nothing wrong with this one? '

> —**Princess Anne,** to a sharp-eyed reporter who pointed out that she had worn a suit of apple green several times before.

★ ★

As Lady Diana Spencer, the future Queen of England was snapped by Lord Snowdon for a fashion feature in *Vogue*. She modelled a blouse designed by the Emanuels.

★ ★

What Lady Diana wore for her official engagement photographs with Prince Charles and the Queen:
A navy blue suit, with a straight skirt and a drawstring-waisted jacket, worn over a white sailor-style shirt trimmed by a scarlet bow. The outfit was finished off by navy blue shoes in punched leather, and the almost obligatory strand of pearls.

★ ★

When Princess Diana began wearing her Catherine Walker 'puff ball' dresses, Prince Charles is said to have enquired of her, 'Why are you wearing a parachute?'

Hat styles favoured by the Princess of Wales include the jaunty tricorn, the veiled pillbox (Prince Charles's favourite), and the wide-brimmed Breton.

★ ★

The Princess of Wales wears size eight shoes.

★ ★

Clothes designers favoured by the Princess of Wales: Arabella Pollen, Bruce Oldfield, Kanga (Dale, Lady Tryon), the Emanuels, Jasper Conran, Caroline Charles, Jan Vanvelden, Catherine Walker.

★ ★

Both the Princess of Wales and the Duchess of York wear Manolo Blahnik shoes; prices start at £100 a pair.

★ ★

Princess Diana caused a stir in the British press on 25 April 1989, when she took Prince Harry to kindergarten wearing baggy sweatshirt, man's jacket, baseball cap and baggy trousers tucked into cowboy boots. The daily TV discussion programme *Kilroy* was prompted to pose the question to its audience, 'Should mothers dress fashionably to take their children to school, or does it embarrass the child?'

★ ★

Fashion gaffes of the Princess of Wales:

Outfit worn to the ballet in Portugal, Feburary 1987. The black taffeta skirt and bow-tie looked marvellous, but the addition of a tangerine satin jacket made more than one observer think she had forgotten to put her shirt on.

That hat worn on her gondola ride through Venice. The last time anything curled up at the edges like that, it was labelled 'British Rail cheese sandwich'.

That black taffeta evening gown worn on her first official public function following the engagement announcement. As anyone who has worn a dress of this design will tell you, you should always check your neckline *before* presenting yourself to the TV cameras.

★ ★

Fashion gaffes of the Duchess of York:

The 'slashed' satin dress of Ascot fame – white, with black, bright green and blue bands across the bodice.

Ascot hat. Variously described as 'a blue flying saucer', 'an upturned fruit basket' and 'one of the Queen Mother's cast-offs,' it was decorated with a huge white carnation stuck to the side as an afterthought.

A black leather mini skirt worn to an evening engagement. Even her father didn't approve, and said so.

Trousers in a large floral print. These may look beautiful on the Princess of Wales, but not on Fergie . . .

★ ★

Clothes designers favoured by Fergie:
Roberto Devorik, Gina Fratini, Suzanne Schneider, Paul Golding, Yves St Laurent, Lindka Ceirach.

★ ★

The Duchess of York does not wear stockings!

★ ★

Fergie rebuffed:
It is well-known that Royals often receive hefty discounts when buying clothes such as ballgowns, simply because the fashion houses involved recognise good publicity when they see it. However, it is usual to wait for the offer of a discount to be made, and then to accept it. The Duchess of York asked Zandra Rhodes for the aforementioned discount, in return for publicity. As one of the world's top designers, Ms Rhodes' reply was short and sweet: 'My darling, I don't *need* the publicity.'

SHOPPING AROUND

Anyone can shop where the Royals buy their goods and services – if they can afford it; though even Royals buy from chain stores sometimes.

Three continuous years of good service are required before a shop, service or company receives a Royal Warrant, with the accompanying privilege of stamping their goods 'By Royal Appointment'. Here are just a few:

★ ★

By Appointment to Her Majesty the Queen:

Harrods – Provisions and household goods.

Collingwood – Silver and jewellery.

Burberrys – Clothing.

Floris – Perfume.

Viyella – Viyella and Sydella fabrics.

Harveys Bristol Cream – Sherry.

Spode – China.

Keith Prowse – Theatre tickets, etc.

★ ★

By Appointment to Her Majesty the Queen Mother:

Harrods – China, glass and fancy goods.

Collingwood – Jewellery.

Burberrys – Clothing.

Keith Prowse – Theatre tickets, etc.

Fortnum and Mason – Provisions.

Aquascutum – Coats and other outerwear.

★ ★

The Queen does still occasionally shop personally at Harrods, but it is done very early in the morning before the store is officially open. The Queen Mother has selections of gifts sent to Clarence House for her perusal.

★ ★

Chain stores which have been favoured by Royalty:
Marks and Spencer – Queen Mary.
Benetton, Mothercare, BhS – Princess Diana.

★ ★

Fortnum and Mason is known as a top people's shop the world over, and is favoured by all members of the Royal Family. It is interesting, therefore, to consider the shop's origins.

Servants have always benefited from certain perks. In the old Hanoverian Courts, one such perk was the privilege of removing wax stubs from the Royal candle holders each morning. Two enterprising servants sold these leftover bits of wax to lesser mortals. With the money thus accumulated, Mr Fortnum and Mr Mason founded their famous shop, and it has continued to serve Royalty ever since.

★ ★

Harrods are Outfitters by Royal Appointment to both the Duke of Edinburgh and the Prince of Wales.

Prince Charles buys his suits and other clothes at Harrods; there is a separate 'store within a store' where he can choose his favourite Turnbull and Asser shirts. Unlike his wife, however, he does not visit the shop during normal opening hours; and the tailor and his assistants call at Kensington Palace to do the fittings.

* *

Gieves & Hawkes in Savile Row, London, make uniforms and other official regalia for State occasions.

* *

Hackett, London, is a frequent choice for Viscount Linley when he's buying clothes.

SEE ANYTHING YOU HAVEN'T GOT ?

Simpson in Piccadilly are Royal Outfitters by Appointment to the Queen, Prince Philip and the Prince of Wales.

★ ★

Princess Diana buys knitwear from Inca The Peruvian Shop, London.

★ ★

The Duchess of York favours Louis Vuitton luggage and travelling accessories.

★ ★

Berry Brothers supply wine to the Court. Simon Berry was an escort of Lady Diana Spencer before she married.

★ ★

Winalot provide the biscuit meal for Royal canines.

★ ★

Prince Andrew buys his photographic equipment from Wallace Heaton, New Bond Street, London, W1.

★ ★

The Duchess of York purchases her skiing equipment from Olympic Way, Harrods.

★ ★

Both Prince William and Prince Harry are fond of their teddies. The Royal bears are dressed in tiny, hand-knitted sweaters, and are sold in Harrods Toy Department.

★ ★

The Duke and Duchess of Kent buy their silver cutlery, salt cellars, etc from Asprey.

★ ★

Where the Yorks kept their wedding gift lists:
The General Trading Company, Thomas Goode & Co., Charles Hammond and Asprey (all in London).

PARTIES AND PRESENTS

What do you buy the Queen Mum for Christmas, Prince Charles for his birthday, or a Royal baby at his or her christening?

The Royal Family open their Christmas presents on Christmas Eve, though the very youngest members still have to wait until morning.

★ ★

Christmas gifts received by Royals in 1989:

Princess Beatrice – Snow suit, brush and comb set.

The Queen – Rose-scented soaps and Corgi-shaped soaps.

Prince Harry – State-of-the art pony tack.

Prince William – BMX bike.

★ ★

The Royal Family hold a competition between themselves at Christmas, to see who can produce the most originally wrapped gifts. Princess Alice of Gloucester usually wins.

★ ★

On Easter Sunday, the older members of the Royal family traditionally give each other pretty pieces of china or porcelain wrapped in tissue paper, rather than Easter eggs, though Princess Diana gives Charles a Suchard egg.

Amusing gifts they have given each other:

Prince Charles to Princess Diana –
A pair of joke plastic breasts, following her complaint that after the births of the princes her bust had disappeared. On unwrapping the gift, she immediately put them on over her dress at the traditional Christmas Eve family party.

Princess Diana to the Queen –
Corgi-shaped soaps from Crabtree & Evelyn.

Young Royals to the Duke and Duchess of York –
A giant teddy bear, seated in their Going Away open landau.

Prince Charles to his parents –
False moustaches and plastic noses, stuffed in old socks.

Sensible gifts they have given each other:

A doormat for Gatcombe Park House –
Prince Charles to his sister

Paintboxes –
Queen Mary to her grandchildren

The Iveagh Tiara –
Queen Mary received it from Queen Victoria, Queen Elizabeth gave it to the Princess of Wales; all received it as a wedding gift

A grey silk nightdress –
Prince Charles to his wife.

★ ★

Small pieces of jewellery, or antique silver items, are the usual gifts presented to a Royal baby at his or her christening. It is also traditional to give a small gift to the child's nanny.

★ ★

Members of the Royal Family receive thousands of letters and cards when a wedding, birthday, new baby or recovery from an illness is celebrated. To differentiate between good wishes of the public and those of the Royals themselves, a secret mark is made by the sender in the top left-hand corner of the envelopes.

★ ★

Animals invited to Royal birthday parties:

A camel – Gave rides to small guests at one of Lady Diana Spencer's childhood parties.

Bee the otter – Sang 'Happy Birthday' to Lady Gabriella Windsor at Kensington Palace.

★ ★

The (reputed) cost of Royal jewels:
The pearl, diamond and emerald necklace given to the Princess of Wales on the arrival of her firstborn son cost an estimated £100,000.

The Duchess of York's cabuchon ruby engagement ring cost £25,000 before setting (or 'engineering', as the Duke of York phrased it).

As Edward VIII, the Duke of Windsor bestowed on Mrs Simpson £50,000 worth of jewels for Christmas, and a further £60,000 for New Year.

The jewels given as personal wedding gifts to Princess Mary of Teck amounted in value to almost a million pounds (and would be worth much more today).

★　★

Things Royals have given to raise funds for charity:

Their patronage.

Their time, and personal appearances.

Private financial donations (exact amounts are strictly confidential).

A pair of white kid pilot's gloves worn by himself during the Falklands War, and labelled 'Slightly soiled'. Given by Prince Andrew to be auctioned for the South Atlantic Fund.

A drawing of Prince William, sketched on board the Royal Yacht _Britannia_ by the Princess of Wales. She allowed its inclusion in a book sold to raise money for children's charities. (Permission was sought, but not given, for the original sketch to be auctioned separately.)

Queen Mary's Doll's House. Fees paid to see it on a nationwide tour went to charities assisting the injured and maimed of the First World War.

★　★

As small children, the Queen and Princess Margaret always made gifts themselves to give friends and family at Christmas and on birthdays. These items included calendars, lino-cut pictures, self-portraits, lavender bags and, in Princess Elizabeth's case, hand-written observations of State occasions noted down in exercise books.

One of the Queen's most precious possessions from childhood is a silver shilling coin. Accompanied by her sister, Princess Elizabeth was taken on an educational visit to the Royal Mint by Queen Mary. A hair from Princess Elizabeth's head was stamped onto the newly minted shilling piece, a memento which she still treasures today.

★ ★

Celebrating VE Night, 1945:
As young princesses, Elizabeth and Margaret anonymously joined the throng of revellers outside Buckingham Palace – and the future Queen of England knocked a policeman's helmet off. Explaining his decision to allow this freedom to his daughters, George VI said, 'With the war and everything, they've never had any fun.'

★ ★

On the occasion of the Queen's twenty-first birthday, the *Sunday Graphic* carried a celebratory poem, by Enid Blyton.

★ ★

The Queen celebrated her twenty-first birthday during the Royal Tour of South Africa in 1947. The South African nation, led by Jan Smuts, presented her with eighty-seven perfect diamonds in a gold casket, at her Coming-of-Age banquet.

★ ★

In 1958, Duke Ellington met the Queen. Afterwards, he wrote the 'Queen's Suite' just for her. A single pressing of the record was made – at Ellington's own request – and no more were to be made until after his death. The musical score was lodged at the American Congress, and in 1988 received its first public performance.

★ ★

Australia's Bicentennial gift to the Queen:
A new State coach.

★ ★

Favourite items of jewellery belonging to the Queen:

Her wedding ring – The inscription inside has never been publicly revealed.

Double-strand pearl necklace – A wedding gift from her father.

Art Deco 'flower basket' brooch – Featuring emeralds for leaves and rubies for flowers; a birthday gift from her parents.

★   ★

Who said . . . ?
‹Good heavens, it's a loin cloth!›
> —**Queen Mary,** on viewing Ghandhi's wedding present to Princess Elizabeth and the Duke of Edinburgh.

★   ★

The Queen likes to give books as gifts: usually non-fiction, thrillers and biographies to Prince Philip and Prince Charles, books on photography to the Duke of York, tomes on bloodstock or dog-breeding to friends. She very much enjoys choosing toys for her grandchildren. Queen Elizabeth herself receives dog leads, scarves, framed photographs, photograph albums, and – in 1982 – a pair of porcelain candlesticks from the Prince and Princess of Wales. She and Prince Philip always receive a stocking of novelties from Prince Charles and Princess Diana.

★   ★

The first Christmas they were married, Prince Charles and Princess Diana gave all the Royals gifts of Dartington Glass.

★   ★

For her twentieth birthday in 1981, Lady Diana Spencer received a solid gold wristwatch and matching bracelet from Prince Charles.

★   ★

113

Favourite items of jewellery belonging to the Princess of Wales:

A gold initial 'D', worn on a neck chain – A birthday present from schoolfriends.

Seed pearl necklace, with a pendant in the shape of the Prince of Wales Feathers fashioned in diamonds and emeralds – a gift from her husband on the birth of Prince William.

The Iveagh Tiara – A wedding gift from her mother-in-law.

A Russian wedding ring in red and white gold – A personal possession from her pre-marriage days.

★ ★

What Princess Diana gives Prince Charles on his birthday and for Christmas:
Silk Dior ties, Italian knitwear, originals of apt cartoons which have appeared in the newspapers.

★ ★

Princess Anne opted for a sailing trip on her father's yacht as a gift for her seventeenth birthday, cruising around the coast of Scotland.

★ ★

The Duchess of Windsor gave Princess Michael of Kent a pair of Cartier panther earrings as a wedding gift.

★ ★

Items from the Duke and Duchess of York's wedding gift list:
Vases by Dartington Glass, solid silver cutlery, Georgian dining table and chairs, eight sofas, coffee mugs decorated with a teddy bear motif, a course of flying lessons (for the Duchess, not the Duke), jewellery (from the Queen), building land (from the Queen).

MAKING HEADLINES

Gentlemen of the press, Court correspondents, Royal journalists or the Rat Pack. Love them or hate them, they chronicle the Royals' every move.

A Gallup Poll conducted on behalf of the *Daily Telegraph* in December 1988 found that the Queen was the person most people wanted to meet (beating Mother Teresa and Michael Jackson), that Princess Diana was considered the most modern and fashionable, and the Princess Royal the most caring of all the Royals. The Duchess of York was, according to those who took part in the survey, vulgar and arrogant.

★ ★

When an employee of the Royal Household decides to tell all to the media or press, their action is known as 'doing a Crawfie', named after Marion Crawford, the Royal nanny who betrayed their trust.

★ ★

Who said . . . ?
❝It would have been a very different story if Prince Philip had been sleeping here. ❞
> —**The Queen,** following the occasion in 1982 when Michael Fagin broke into her bedroom. This piece of information – that she and the Duke of Edinburgh have separate bedrooms – supposedly rocked the nation. It didn't.

‘I am in love with a woman named Elizabeth Regina. ’
> —What Michael Fagin reputedly said to his wife. He also said that the 'woman' was married, with four children.

★ ★

‘That'll teach you to spill my whisky. ’
> —**The Queen** to a press photographer. At a reception he had dropped his drink on the carpet in front of her, then the flash on his camera failed. Hence her comment.

★ ★

Merry Christmas:
The Queen's Speech on TV and Radio always used to be broadcast live. This meant that Her Majesty was so nervous she could not eat the family Christmas lunch. Nowadays it is recorded well in advance.

★ ★

Who said . . . ?
‘I hope to God that he breaks his bloody neck. ’
> —**Prince Philip,** after a particularly persistent photographer shinned up a flagpole and lost his grip, on the Royal trip to India in 1961.

★ ★

Of whom was it said . . . ?
‘Not the most tactful man I've ever met. ’
> —**Prince Philip,** by a member of the Press Corps on the 1986 Royal tour of China.

★ ★

The Duke of Edinburgh wrote and delivered the 1989 Dimbleby Lecture, entitled 'Living Off the Land', putting conservation into its global context.

★ ★

Who said . . . ?

'And a particularly nasty one [New Year] to your Editors. '
>—**Prince Charles** to a gaggle of pressmen, who had descended on Sandringham.

★ ★

'I didn't know . . . '
>—**Princess Michael of Kent,** on the publication of her late father's wartime activities.

★ ★

Who was called . . . ?

'The Royal Wimp of Windsor. '
>—**Prince Edward,** by a US newspaper. He had just quit the Royal Marines.

★ ★

Who referred to the world's press as *'Reptiles '?*
>—**Major Ronald Ferguson.** They were waiting at the Guards Polo Club, Windsor, when he arrived for his first polo match after the scandal concerning his visit to a club of dubious reputation.

★ ★

'Can't she send a servant out to buy them for her? '
>—A Fleet Street Editor, one of a group called to the Palace following pre-wedding incidents when Lady Diana Spencer was pursued by the press on her way to buy sweets.

★ ★

And a Royal re-buff . . .

'That is the most pompous thing I've ever heard! '
>—**The Queen,** to the aforementioned Fleet Street Editor, just before she stalked out of the room in disgust.

★ ★

'Do you want to know the colour of my bloomers?'
> —**Lady Diana Spencer,** on being pursued into Janet Reger's lingerie shop by pressmen.

* *

'I thought you must have been lying on the ground looking up my skirt.'
> —Again, the **Princess of Wales.** The press was continuing its strange preoccupation with the colour and style of her underwear.

* *

During her first autumn holiday at Balmoral after becoming Princess of Wales, the British tabloid press took great pleasure in reporting that Diana, along with other members of the Royal Family, had taken part in a deer stalk and had actually 'felled a stag with a single shot'. If there is one thing Princess Diana will never, ever do, it is take an active part in bloodsports. Not surprisingly, she was both angered and distressed by the media coverage.

During the visit of the Princess of Wales to New York in February 1989, a newspaper article described the ensuing 'Dimania' as 'a benign malady . . .'.

★ ★

The Duchess of York was featured on the front cover of the *Sunday Times Magazine* in July 1987. Inside was a feature entitled 'Move Over, Diana'.

★ ★

The Duchess of York's *Budgie the Helicopter* books were voted 'The Stupidest of the Year' by American critics.

★ ★

Four major British TV series about Royalty:
Elizabeth R, Edward VII, Edward and Mrs Simpson, The Six Wives of Henry VIII.

★ ★

Two feature films about Royalty:

A Royal Love Story – Based on the romance of Prince Charles and Princess Diana, and starring Catherine Oxenburg (who is in fact a several-times-removed cousin of Prince Philip).

A King's Story – About the Duke and Duchess of Windsor. They attended the film's Paris premiere in 1966.

★ ★

On 26th March 1990 Viscount Linley, son of Princess Margaret, became the first member of the Royal family to bring a libel action to court.

The *Today* newspaper's daily gossip column had recorded that, while in the 'Ferret and Firkin' public house, in Chelsea, Viscount Linley had poured beer over customers and furniture, and behaved 'like an upper-class lager lout.' The paper claimed he had then been banned from the pub. He was awarded damages of £35,000, but the next day he stated that he would only accept £5,000 because he had made his point.

THE FINAL CHAPTER

F *amous last words appear to be mainly the preserve of politicians, who even with their dying breath still seem to get the final word in; perhaps the Royals are simply too well brought up.*

Queen Alexandra died at Sandringham not Clarence House, as is often claimed.

★ ★

It comes as no surprise to learn that King George IV died when he did. His death certificate lists dropsy, gout, cirrhosis of the liver, nephritis and ruptured abdominal blood vessels as the cause of his demise. Presumably the Royal physicians were too polite to state that he had drunk himself to death.

★ ★

Immediately after the death of Prince Albert, Queen Victoria rushed to the nursery where her youngest child was sleeping. Wrapping the child in Prince Albert's dressing gown, she took Princess Beatrice to sleep in her own bed.

★ ★

Edward VIII accused Lord Dawson, Royal Physician, of murdering George V.

★ ★

The public hangman, who also had the job of beheading Charles I and was paid £30 to commit regicide, was Gregory Brandon, and he lived in Rosemary Lane, Whitechapel.

★ ★

Perhaps the saddest of Royal deaths in modern times was that of George VI in 1952. His wife, Queen Elizabeth (now the Queen Mother), and Princess Margaret had retired to bed after a day spent cruising the Norfolk Broads while the King had been out shooting on the Sandringham estate. Princess Elizabeth was in Kenya. King George read in bed for a while, drinking his cocoa. A member of staff walking through the garden saw him close his bedroom window and draw the curtains. That was the last time anyone saw him alive. He died in the quiet of the night, alone. No famous last words or deathbed speeches, just a weary body letting go its spirit.

★ ★

After the death of George VI, a close family friend commented to the Queen Mother that she appeared to be bearing up well. The Queen Mother's reply belied her brave face: 'Only in public, my dear. In private it is a very different story.'

★ ★

At the annual Remembrance Day services, the Queen Mother has great cause to remember. In the First World War, her eldest brother Fergus was killed while leading his Scottish Regiment into battle.

In 1944 her nephew, Patrick, the young Master of Glamis, lost his life when leading the same Regiment.

Her brother-in-law, the Duke of Kent, was killed while serving with the RAF in 1942. She places a cross in the Westminster Garden of Remembrance every year on 11 November.

★ ★

Lord Mountbatten's favourite hymn:
'For Those in Peril on the Sea'. He chose it as part of his funeral service.

★ ★

'The only sad thing, Charles, is that I won't be there to enjoy it. '
> —**Lord Louis Mountbatten** to his 'Honorary Grandson', Prince Charles, about the funeral he had planned for himself.

★ ★

On the wreath Prince Charles sent to the funeral of Lord Louis Mountbatten, the plain white card bore a simple and poignant message: 'To my H.G.F. from his H.G.S.' – 'To my Honorary Grandfather from his Honorary Grandson'.

★ ★

Who said . . . ?
'God takes the good first. '
> —**The Duchess of York,** about the death of Major Hugh Lindsay at Klosters, speaking to staff at St Andrew's Hospice in Airdrie, Scotland, where she was on an official visit.

CROWNING GLORY

Pomp, circumstance, pageantry – a Coronation has it all. What a shame they can't be held more often!

At the crowning of every monarch, the Archbishop of Canterbury offers up . . . 'the most valuable thing that this world affords'. That 'most valuable thing' is the Holy Bible.

★ ★

The ring placed on the finger of the monarch during the Coronation ceremony is called 'The wedding ring of England'.

★ ★

Who says . . . ?
‹With this Sword do justice. ›
   —The Archbishop of Canterbury, at the Coronation
    of each monarch.

★ ★

The Coronation of Queen Victoria was not without its memorable moments. One of the most spectacular was when the new monarch spotted an altar in a side chapel being used as an impromptu picnic table. . . . No, she was not amused.

★ ★

Twenty thousand Americans poured into London for the Coronation of George VI.

★ ★

Edward V, like Edward VII, was never crowned.

⋆ ⋆

During the Second World War, the rumour began circulating that the Stone of Scone, which stands beneath the Coronation Chair in Westminster Abbey, had been despatched to Canada for safe-keeping. It was, in fact, buried beneath the floor of the Islip Chapel – just a few feet from its normal position.

⋆ ⋆

In preparation for the 1953 Coronation of Queen Elizabeth II, the *Daily Sketch* carried centre-page photographic portraits of major Royals, including Prince Charles and Princess Anne. Queen Mary's picture was also much in evidence, though she died shortly before the Coronation took place. At the aged Queen's request, the Coronation was not postponed.

⋆ ⋆

To watch the Coronation procession of Elizabeth II people paid up to £50 for a seat in the stands and £3,500 for a view from an office window or balcony.

⋆ ⋆

Who said . . . ?
'Pray for me on that day.'
    —**The Queen,** speaking during the Christmas broadcast prior to her Coronation.

⋆ ⋆

Like her great-great-grandmother, Queen Elizabeth II felt so sick on the morning of her Coronation that she couldn't eat her breakfast.

⋆ ⋆

'I think she did very well.'
    —**The Duke of Windsor,** after watching the Coronation of his niece Elizabeth on TV.

JOKES AND JAPES

In Belgium it's a crime to joke publicly about the Royal Family. Thankfully, it isn't in Britain.

Generations of Royalty have enjoyed – or endured – the annual Royal Variety Show. Queen Mary would show displeasure if jokes were too risqué or made fun of the opera – her snorts of disapproval could be clearly heard by those occupying neighbouring boxes at the theatre. George V, on the other hand, would laugh like a drain.

★ ★

Spitting Image, a satirical television series, depicts . . .

The Duchess of York as a snorting buck-toothed, red-haired hyperactive Royal in a sheepskin flying jacket . . .

The Princess of Wales as a Barbie Doll Sloane . . .

The Prince of Wales as a philosophising upper-class twit, with elephantine ears . . .

And the Queen Mother as a gin-swigging lady landowner with a Yorkshire accent.

★ ★

On one Royal Tour, a large banner proclaimed 'God Save the Queen!' Underneath had been added 'And God Help The Consort'. A delighted Prince Philip photographed it for his private collection.

Who said . . . ?

'That looks to me like something to hang a towel on. '

—**Prince Philip,** on _Relief Construction_ by Victor Passmore, on show in San Francisco's Museum of Art.

★ ★

Who said to Anne, Princess Royal . . . ?

'The last time I made a speech it was in the High Court. '

—A long-term prisoner in Scotland's top-security Barlinnie Jail. He had just presented her with a gold and silver brooch made in the prison workshops; the Princess Royal appreciated the joke very much.

★ ★

Who said . . . ?

'Oh look, darling – they're trying to save us! '

—**Diana to Charles,** after spotting a 'Save The Whales' poster. The Prince didn't laugh.

'He never laughs at my jokes.'
—**Princess Diana,** speaking of her husband.

* *

'They're playing our song.'
—**Prince Charles** to Diana, during the playing of the National Anthem. Her Majesty was not amused.

* *

'You mustn't get caught speeding in that.'
—**Prince Charles,** to a wheelchair-bound pensioner, during a visit to the Scilly Isles.

* *

'Good grief, he's not the Pope, you know.'
—**Princess Diana.** When the Royal parents took baby Prince William to Australia, photographers complained that his feet had not touched Australian soil – his mother had carried him down the aircraft steps.

* *

'Charles says it's in the dress.'
—**The Princess of Wales** to an elderly man in that country, who had asked why, when her dress was in the colours of the Welsh flag, the dragon – symbol of Wales – was missing from the design.

* *

A cartoon in a British daily newspaper depicted the Prince and Princess of Wales sitting on a Spanish beach, watching their sons build sand castles – each 'castle' bore a flag labelling it as Balmoral, Buckingham Palace or Kensington Palace. The Royal parents were saying, 'Oh *do* stop showing off!'

* *

‹I'm sorry, but Diana's beaten you to it. ›
> —A British newspaper cartoonist; someone had just called him to ask if he could acquire the original of a cartoon, depicting Prince Charles talking to his plants.

★ ★

‹When Britain wins a battle she shouts "God Save the Queen"; when she loses, she votes down the Prime Minister. ›
> — **Sir Winston Churchill**

★ ★

The Royal Tour of South Africa took place in 1947, in an atmosphere of continuing tension between the British and the Afrikaners, which had been festering since the Boer War in Queen Victoria's reign.

During a walkabout, a belligerent Afrikaner addressed Queen Elizabeth (now the Queen Mother) and told her how badly his people had been treated by the English. The Queen looked at the man and, wearing her most charming smile, replied 'I do so understand. We Scots feel exactly the same.'

★ ★

Who said . . . . ?
‹Somebody kiss it and it will turn into a prince. ›
> —**Prince Charles.** In 1981 whilst planting a tree, a frog jumped over his foot.